D1602041

RYAN McGINNESS

SPONSORSHIP

The Fine Art of Corporate Sponsorship

The Corporate Sponsorship of Fine Art

GINGKO PRESS

SPONSORSHIP

The Fine Art of Corporate Sponsorship

The Corporate Sponsorship of Fine Art

Essays by

Shepard Fairey
Adam Glickman
Carlo McCormick
Jacqui Millar
Steve Powers (ESPO)
Rob Walker

By Ryan McGinness

*Published on the Occasion
of the Exhibition "Sponsorship"
at BLK/MRKT Gallery,
Los Angeles, 2003*

Interviews with

Tony Arcabascio (SITE)
Craig Costello (KR)
DALEK
EASE
David Ellis (SKWERM)
Brendan Fowler (BARR)
FUTURA
GREEN LADY
Evan Hecox
Matt Houston
Rich Jacobs
Todd James (REAS)
Chris Johanson
KAWS
Young Kim
Barry McGee (TWIST)
Bill McMullen
Christian Strike
Romon Yang (RO-STARR)

SPONSORSHIP
The Fine Art of Corporate Sponsorship
The Corporate Sponsorship of Fine Art
RYAN MCGINNESS

PUBLISHED BY
GINGKO PRESS, INCORPORATED
5768 PARADISE DRIVE, SUITE J
CORTE MADERA, CA 94925
GINGKOPRESS.COM

ISBN: 1-58423-199-8

PUBLISHED IN THE USA IN 2005
PRINTED AND BOUND IN HONG KONG

THIS BOOK WAS ORIGINALLY PUBLISHED IN 2003
IN AN EDITION OF 1,000 BY ANTHEM BOOKS &
OBEY GIANT ART, INC. ON THE OCCASION OF
THE EXHIBITION *RYAN MCGINNESS: SPONSORSHIP*
AT BLK/MRKT GALLERY IN LOS ANGELES.

ANTHEM-MAGAZINE.COM
OBEYGIANT.COM
BLKMRKTGALLERY.COM

BOOK PRODUCERS:
DUSTIN BEATTY & AMANDA FAIREY
EXHIBITION PRODUCER: AMANDA FAIREY
PROJECT COORDINATOR: GRACE HSIU
AUDIO TRANSCRIPTION: GEORGE BUNCE

Contents

■

■

There seem to be two reactions people have when they see artwork that they like: they either respectfully support it and want to share it with others, or they attempt to co-opt its ownership and figure out a way to profit from it. Since the original publication of this book in 2003, this dichotomy has become even more clear to me. Like many of the artists I interviewed, I've had extremely positive experiences with people who like my work and extremely negative experiences with people who like my work. Consequently, I've been able to realize numerous projects, installations, and exhibitions that have helped me grow and make better work. However, I've also had to file a lawsuit against a snowboard company for changing and publishing my artwork on a snowboard; I've had to terminate a licensing agreement with a company that enthusiastically produced products without my permission; and I've had to track down a company in Japan that removed a mural I created in a gallery in Tokyo and sold it to a retail store. From undelivered royalty reports to unfulfilled promises and unreturned artwork, it sometimes seems like it doesn't pay to make well-received work. Perhaps I should feel lucky that people care enough about my work to steal it in the first place.

The question I've been asked most regarding this book is if I hate corporations. I don't hate corporations. In fact, I own two, and I've been a part owner of numerous corporations since I learned how to play the stock market when I was 15. I don't hate corporations, because with a corporation, there is nothing to hate. Hate is an emotion, and corporations are soul-less entities incapable of receiving or reciprocating any emotion. When dealing with

corporations, one needs to behave like a corporation, treating these corporate relationships unlike any personal relationships you may have with the people within the organization. Corporations are simply legal entities, despite their sometimes valiant efforts to humanize themselves. One such effort that is increasingly popular is for a corporation to involve itself with artists. After all, making art is probably the most human of all activities. While the goal of an artist is to focus him- or herself in an effort to make great work, great work takes time to make. And time is money. Since the primary goal of a corporation is to make money, there's a natural link there. With my positive experiences in mind, I still have faith that this natural link can be nurtured and that successful relationships can be created between man and machine.

To build a successful relationship, though, my suggestion is for artists to work only with corporations that are willing to step into the artist's world and be a part of the artist's program rather than have the artist submit to the corporate agenda. Re-reading this book after two years, I found that Donald Sultan had the best piece of advice concerning this approach. He explains, "You don't have to make your art fit so much as find a way for everything else to fit around it."

RYAN MCGINNESS, 2005

■

■

*When I was 14 years old, I couldn't afford a new
skateboard. So I wrote to all my favorite skateboard
companies and told them I was hosting a skate
contest in my hometown of Virginia Beach. I asked
them to donate prizes for my contest. A few weeks
later, I received a huge Powell Peralta skull banner,
Bones Brigade t-shirts, Santa Cruz Rob Roskop
decks, and numerous stickers. I also received t-shirts
from a variety of other companies. I never held the
event; I just divided the booty up among my friends.*

*The lessons I learned were complex. The effort I put
into the presentation of my pitch letter (which
mimicked corporate correspondence I had found in
junk mail laying around the house) was rewarded,
and I quickly understood the deceitful power of
design. The skateboard companies I approached were
looking to support a grass-roots effort by using local
events as advertising vehicles, and I figured out how
to exploit their agenda.*

*I didn't draw a distinction between small, private,
bootstrapped companies trying to do the right thing
and large corporations only out for profit. When
you're a teenager growing up in suburbia, the whole
world is your enemy. Now only most of the world
is my enemy, and I created the "Sponsorship" exhibition and this book to help discover why this is.*

RYAN MCGINNESS, 2003

■

■

Introduction

In the Fall of 2001, Tony Arcabascio of Alife told me about his concept for an empty retail space. The idea was not to sell products but instead to provide the service of distributing information in the form of giveaway products and promotional items for those individuals and companies that paid to have their messages on display. This pay-to-play model would operate on a scale. Large corporations would pay more to display their advertising messages, while individuals would pay less to share their messages with the public in the same space. This advertising-as-content would be curated, not open to just anyone and everyone. Consequently, the public would come to trust that this space was the spot to go to find out about the latest new music, restaurants, clothes, etc. The space would become a brand itself, symbiotically supported by select sponsors.

Since our initial discussion, Tony has evolved this concept with his partners at Alife by substituting the pay-to-play model with a purely curatorial one. Within their retail environment, they work with select larger corporations (and only with select products) while showcasing the work of emerging companies and artists. Their curatorial approach ensures that both ends of the spectrum co-exist on a level playing field, and the public has come to expect a higher standard from Alife.

BLK/MRKT similarly applies the Robin Hood approach to the service industry. Founded by artists who sought commercial applications for their work, BLK/MRKT seeks relationships with large corporations so it can afford to support and showcase fine art through its gallery.

Many of the artists exhibiting in spaces like Alife and BLK/MRKT are moving beyond this simple sponsorship model by co-branding themselves with corporations for various projects (with shoes, clothing, figures, etc.). This is a new paradigm: a two-way patronage unique to our generation. Artists are generating financial support for their own work instead of relying on grants from governments, families, or institutions. In return, companies get the street/art/subculture credibility that builds their brands. All of these models are being replicated at a furious pace as more and more corporations strive to be down with youth culture, creative agencies curate and author their own content, and artists seek increasingly broad audiences. As a reaction to these trends, I did not produce any work for the *Sponsorship* exhibition. Instead, I set up a sponsorship program whereby any company could contribute any amount it wished in cash, products, or services. The sponsors' logos were on display at different sizes and locations (commensurate with their level of contribution), along with product and promotional giveaways. My hope was that an empty exhibition would create enough pause for us to consider both the fine art of corporate sponsorship and the corporate sponsorship of fine art.

This book is a collection of essays and interviews I conducted with various artists about this emerging trend of sponsorship in the visual arts.

I heartfully dedicate this book to the artists who spent their valuable time with me as we tried to tackle this issue.

■

■

Essays

"A great example is L.L. Cool J's Gap commercial. In the ad, he dropped the name of a competing clothing line with which he was affiliated. In the ad, his words 'for us, by us' referenced FUBU clothing, but Gap didn't figure out the coup until it was too late."

Shepard Fairey

Shepard Fairey

Graphic artist Shepard Fairey lives in Los Angeles. He is the founder of the Obey Giant sticker and poster campaign and co-founder of design firm BLK/MRKT, Inc. Shepard designs billboards by day and liberates them at night. (obeygiant.com)

The other day I was flipping through a "lifestyle" magazine when an Absolut Vodka ad caught my eye. This particular ad was basically a verbatim reproduction of the classic *Never Mind the Bollocks, Here's the Sex Pistols* cover, with the sole modification to the original Jamie Reid art being a cut paper style Absolut bottle silhouette behind the Sex Pistols type, instead of the usual simple rectangle. The type at the bottom of the page read "Absolut Pistols" in the typestyle they have branded for years. At first, I had my typical Pavlovian response of jubilation at seeing a Sex Pistols graphic. The Sex Pistols are close to my heart as an important step in the evolution of who I've become today. As what I was seeing really started to sink in, my emotions became more mixed. In a sense, an Absolut ad is a definitive statement of someone's or something's pop culture significance. In this regard, I was pleased that the Pistols had finally reached a certain level of mainstream critical mass. Yet, it was for this exact same reason that the ad made me uneasy. The Sex Pistols used to be very "outsider" and "dangerous," the very album cover being endorsed had been banned 25 years prior. An ad for a very established company is not too punk. I thought to myself, "Would I have looked at the Pistols differently if their Anarchy tour had been the Absolut Anarchy tour?" Maybe not, because The Pistols were the originators of the *Great Rock 'n' Roll Swindle*, but who knows? (Historical note: The Sex Pistols were paid advances by both A&M and EMI records and were promptly dropped for being too controversial before finally settling at Virgin records. Whether or not it was intentional, The Pistols made a decent chunk of money without doing much work until they reached Virgin.)

Back to my point: This essay is about *Sponsorship*, so let me be more specific about how sponsorship relates to The Pistols. The Sex Pistols certainly knew how to work the press, but by keeping chaos high in the mix, sponsorship by a corporation was not even an option. As the Absolut Pistols ad demonstrates, things have changed since those days.

On the surface, sponsorship is a fairly simple relationship; however, the true outcome of sponsorship is determined by an often-unpredictable web of social constructs and perpetually shifting variables. Culture is constantly shifting, not always in the ways one might prefer, but evolving/devolving nonetheless. Would Absolut have taken the chance to endorse the Sex Pistols 25 years ago at the height of their controversy? Maybe not, but today corporations have learned the marketing value of aligning themselves with things that are cutting edge, rebellious, and even controversial. Bands, actors, athletes, artists, and anyone else who has the potential to influence popular culture will be presented with corporate sponsorship opportunities. It is a calculated risk to sponsor someone or something controversial, and corporations sometimes withdraw from a sponsorship agreement if they feel an artist's negative publicity could be damaging to their brand. Even with an album at the top of the charts, R. Kelly would be lucky to find a sponsor, due to his recent indiscretions. Ludacris lost his Pepsi sponsorship for behavior that fell wide of the "family values" target. Today's sponsorship game is high stakes. Though controversy may sell rap records, it still may not offset the financial rewards Ludacris was offered by Pepsi.

Webster's dictionary defines a sponsor as "a business that finances a program in return for advertising" and "a godparent." These are two different definitions, but in some instances sponsorship can provide both. Ideally, sponsorship benefits both parties and compromises neither. However, sponsorship often connotes backroom dealings, hidden agendas, and an overall loss of credibility for the person or group being sponsored. Some partnerships are more logical than others. Sporting goods companies sponsoring athletes makes sense and is well accepted. When it comes to companies sponsoring art shows, the art crowd seems to have greater reservations, no matter how genuinely altruistic the company's motives are. My theory on the hyper-scrutiny of sponsorship within the art community has to do with the idea that true art has no master but the artist. With art, the viewer wants purity, free of compromise, which is difficult to find anywhere else in society. Since the introduction of Pop Art, and the entrance into the Post-Modern era, the only distinction between "fine" and "commercial" art is not style but intent. The idea that art is the artist's personal vision, in no way tainted by a corporate agenda, is central to the definition of "fine" art.

Most artists would probably prefer to avoid sponsorship and the related issues it raises. Some artists have no choice but to use sponsorship to facilitate projects that could not happen otherwise. Artists are compelled to produce their work by any means necessary. Sometimes this solution is as simple and earnest as "This art show was made possible by a generous contribution from Company X." Sometimes the solution requires an artist to negotiate shark-infested waters. And sometimes the artist's methods and agenda can be as covert as the corporation's. A great example is L.L. Cool J's Gap commercial. In the ad he dropped the name of a competing clothing line with which he was affiliated. In the ad, his words "for us, by us" referenced FUBU clothing, but Gap didn't figure out the coup until it was too late. Self-deprecating humor and honesty can also improve the public's perception of a sponsorship. For an art show I did in Philadelphia, which Urban Outfitters wanted to sponsor, I actually designed the flyer to make the sponsorship aspect a conceptual asset. Paying homage to the Sex Pistols, the masters of the "Swindle," I complemented the Urban Outfitters logo on the flyer with the text "Cash for chaos provided by Urban Outfitters." Urban had paid for my trip to Philly, where I would, of course, post my images in the street illegally. Willingly or unwillingly, Urban were my facilitators and accomplices. Sponsorship can be a compromise for an artist due purely to the public's opinion and not to actual pressure from the sponsor to cater to their agenda. A perfect example of this phenomenon involves a poster I did for a show that DC Shoes sponsored. DC is a very respected "core" company, but the poster from my show, which included a half-inch DC logo, sold less briskly, even at a lower price than an identical poster I released later. Some people obviously aren't comfortable with, or at least prefer not to see, the mix of art and corporation.

When Ryan McGinness brought BLK/MRKT his proposal for *Sponsorship*, I thought it was brilliant because it was so simple. Ryan's idea reduced sponsorship to a purely reflexive equation with the artist removed entirely except for his role as "project director." There were no smoke and mirrors, or art for that matter—just a display of logos and products whose hierarchy within the gallery was determined by their associated sponsor's level of contribution. The sponsors were given a description of what the show entailed upfront. To their credit, most wanted to be part of this self-parodying idea without knowing how it might be received by the public. As unconventional an art show as this was, facets of the company's sponsorship goals would still be served. The logos received prominent placement, and the hip tastemaker crowd was treated with a euphoric evening, complete with free booze and multiple free products with which to associate the logos present. If that weren't enough to satisfy the sponsors, Keanu Reaves was allegedly staggering around in a drunken stupor just before the evening's notoriety was sealed by the intrusion of the fire marshal. The very book in which this essay appears was funded by the sponsors and continues to place them in front of people long after the *Sponsorship* art show has ended.

The *Sponsorship* art show succeeded because the sponsors themselves had no control over the show, except to participate or decline. The sponsors involved were not afraid to embrace a good coup, even at their own expense (or they weren't paying attention to what the show was about). Ryan's *Sponsorship* art show reminds us that the attraction to art and artists in the first place is often their freshness, passion, unpredictability, and ability to challenge the status quo. Sponsors who embrace this beautiful chaos head on are the likely leaders of the next commercial generation. The National Endowment for the Arts is basically dead, so sponsorship is likely to play an even more prominent role in the lives of exhibiting artists.

Artists: give the companies credit for taking risks. Companies: give the artists money for taking risks. Everybody wins in this equation.

"Just as Napster did to the music industry and Drudge Report did to network news, a group of young art punks armed with their own, new routes of distribution are unknowingly beginning to challenge the relevance of the art world's system."

Adam Glickman

Adam Glickman

My Peer Cred Weighs a Ton

Adam Glickman is the publisher and owner of the international culture magazine Tokion, *which is based in Manhattan and Tokyo.* Tokion *formally recognized this group of like-minded artists with its seminal "Disobedients" issue in the Spring of 2002. (tokionusa.com)*

It's naïve to insinuate that it can't be real art if there's a Red Bull logo underneath. As long as there has been an established system of art—with sellers and buyers—there's been a firmly set system of sponsorship in place. Fine art has never been a populist pursuit. It's an insiders' industry supported by wealthy patrons and maintained by over-educated curators.

But that's all starting to change. Just as Napster did to the music industry and Drudge Report did to network news, a group of young art punks armed with their own, new routes of distribution are unknowingly beginning to challenge the relevance of the art world's system. Rather than wait for the establishment's recognition, these artists distribute their art through tee shirts, stickers, album covers, the bottom of skateboard decks, graffiti on walls, etc. Through their self-improvised system of distribution, they've allowed thousands, rather than a cultured few, to see their art. Cheaper manufacturing of these goods as well as savvy self-promotion has, for the first time, made it realistic to get one's art out to the world.

It's highly relevant that this is a group of artists who came of age in an era that's going to be remembered as the Golden Age of Marketing. Looking back 30 years from now, we'll probably belly laugh at the obnoxiously obvious branding culture in which people willingly and actively spent their hard-earned money to advertise corporations. This group of artists grew up watching this strange conformist culture grow from an outsider's perspective, and many started their art careers as an ironic poke at it. It's also no coinci-

dence that almost every one of these artists in question came from either a graffiti or skateboarding background. They are natural outsiders, but outsiders with a natural understanding and comfort with the concept of marketing themselves and their art.

And this is where the yukky conflicts of interest begin to appear.

In the '90s, corporate sponsors began spending millions to appear un-corporate. Being in was out. Be 'normal' and you run the risk of coming off like an antagonist from a John Hughes movie: things like 'rich, attractive, popular' were for the first time a sudden no-no. (A favorite example of this is GW Bush, the ultimate insider, who ran a winning campaign by branding himself as an outsider and an underdog.) Just as fast food chains managed to make greasy reheated french fries taste so delicious, marketing and selling rebellion has been scientifically perfected.

This new batch of artists realize this. They've grown up around the branding BS and see the dangers of having their art turned into bubblegum ad campaigns. When MTV's current crop of punk bands are only one step removed from boy bands and rappers only rhyme about fancy champagne and hot tub parties, it's clear that the marketing has overpowered the message.

For this reason, many young artists are reluctant to admit that their tee shirts, stickers, album covers, etc, are "art." Their true art is saved for the canvases. The graffiti, stickers, and tee shirts are just marketing for their gallery work. This is a convenient answer, but I don't really think it's an honest one. Their response, I imagine, comes from that underlying desire to keep the art from being labeled. Its an admirable self-preservation of their scene, because once some journalist or critic (like myself) can manage to define the art, then it begins to confine the art, and once your work can be labeled or defined, then it can be manufactured and repackaged. And no real artists want their artwork to become fodder for next year's Levi's campaign.

Carlo McCormick

Carlo McCormick lives in New York City, writes on popular culture and curates art exhibitions. He is Senior Editor of Paper Magazine. *An edited version of this essay originally appeared in* Paper *in the Sping of 2003. (papermag.com)*

Call it "the fine art of corporate sponsorship," or vice versa: "the corporate sponsorship of fine art," but what has long been a latent tendency in the arts of seeking patronage in unlikely places has recently exploded into a veritable gold rush of opportunity as major corporations, fashion houses, design firms and advertising companies are partnering up with contemporary artists. And while there is some lineage to the conjunction of art, design and commerce—from the modernist masters who did the labels for wine bottles and the Absolut ad campaign of the Eighties to Warhol's myriad commercial projects and Haring's Pop Shop—what is rapidly emerging now is a whole new level of interface in which industry and art are working hand in hand to co-brand products.

Post-Modernism may have inured our jaded palates to the spectacle of seeing corporate logos and consumer goods repositioned as art, and it is now common to find a list of multi-national sponsors attached to most major museum exhibitions, but the very idea that someone would have the utter gall to mount a show called *Sponsorship,* in which the only visual elements were paid corporate advertisements is, well, disturbing to say the least. Such an overt display of fiscal back-scratching, however, is not some vulgar anachronism to our current cultural climate; it is the conceptual embodiment of a new paradigm. With such heavily branded names like Calvin Klein, H&M, Levi's, Nike, Neiman Marcus, Coca Cola, Honda, Tylenol and Adidas commissioning artists to help define their products, there is an emerging cultural climate that offers

great promise as well as peril.

For many with firmly established careers in the art world, teaming up with high-level mass-manufacture offers a chance to work in a variety of new media and creative processes. For a generation of younger artists, however, the ever-widening frontier of artist branding is a complete alternative unto itself, a way of paying bills and getting one's art out there that completely circumvents the gallery system. Ryan McGinness created *Sponsorship* to directly address the current symbiosis between corporations and artists. "A lot of artists are seeking out relationships with corporations as a new way to fund production based on co-authorship," McGinness explains. "They don't want to write grant applications, and besides, there's so little money allocated for the arts; corporations are the last frontier of funding."

For an artist like David Ellis, who in 1999 founded a loose collective of graffiti artists called the Barnstormers that travel yearly down to his rural hometown in North Carolina to paint the local barns, chicken coops, shacks and eighteen wheelers, the optimum exposure of pairing the Barnstormers with the international retail chain H&M is a revelation. "I don't think of myself or the Barnstormers as having gotten much mass attention before. How do these people find us and then talk their clients into doing projects like this? I'm blown away." The focus of H&M's entire Spring campaign, the Barnstormers not only produced a major exhibition in H&M's Soho outlet, but posed themselves prominently in their national advertising campaign. Describing it as a

"What is rapidly emerging now is a whole new level of interface in which industry and art are working hand-in-hand to co-brand products."

Carlo McCormick

learning experience, when Ellis confesses "I need to say no to some shit for a while, to keep a lower profile," it may be less an issue of his art than the ramifications of modeling for ads.

Joakim Gim, the US director of marketing for Sweden-based H&M, sees "a good match in connecting the Barnstormers with our younger line audience." What Gim regards as a self-evident "simple strategy" is, however, deeply layered. Hanging in the aesthetic balance for a program as big as this is both H&M's decision to use real people instead of models as well as their own sensitivity to be "careful of misuse, not overly commercial, and respectful of the artists' integrity." RoStarr, one Barnstormer who did not model in this campaign, was sponsored last year by the shoe company Gravis. As the only artist sponsored in an action industry that regularly strikes such deals with pro skaters, surfers and snow boarders, RoStarr came away "feeling really over-exposed." Still working both as a commercial graphic designer and fine artist, RoStarr maintains "there is something to be gained, but this kind of sponsorship is new, for us as well as the companies. I've branded myself since I was young. I'm my own propagandist. Everything is test-marketed, and I don't think there are many who know the right way to do it."

Luis Calderin, who as marketing manager at Gravis has overseen a number of limited-edition creative footwear series with artists like Stash, Futura, Phil Frost, SSur, Kostas and Ricky Powell, admits "neither RoStarr or I knew what we were getting into. Artists have to keep a certain level of street credibility; they don't want to blow themselves out. After a year run, we agreed that sponsoring him as we would an athlete was not the best way to go. He was an ambassador of the brand who endorsed and helped us with design, but as he was also being constantly approached by other companies, I think he passed up a lot of opportunities in that time." Yasemin Oktay, who as marketing director at Etnies sees the mission as "finding artists within the action-sports genre to bring art into our product," explains from an industry standpoint why there might be this recent wealth of opportunity: "Working with artists can help legitimize a brand within a community of consumers, and when it's done credibly, what it really influences is that small population of people, the taste-makers, who recognize these things."

Shepard Fairey, the prolific and beloved author of the global street art campaigns, *Obey* and *Giant*, who continues to operate a clothing company, a fine-art poster line and the Los Angeles–based design company BLK/MRKT, is certainly among the most successful at navigating the divergent and conflicting opportunities of corporate, fine art and street cultures. Applying the lessons of the latter to big business, Fairey maintains that product appeal "doesn't necessarily have to do anymore with how many units can be sold in the initial six-week period. People can be turned off by solicitation and respond to ambiguity. Art can fester and marinate in people's imaginations, and some companies are slowly starting to get that. You can see how confident marketing, where you hire people to do something that's not just the watered-down crap of most big agencies, pays off." Not by chance, it was Fairey's gallery BLK/MRKT, where McGinness found home for the disembodied artvertising of the *Sponsorship* exhibition. Whether he's fixing up Earthlink after the likes of Chiat Day, helping BMW brand their Mini Cooper, or appearing in Apple computers' 'switch to Mac' campaign, Fairey understands that "Sponsorship is the nature of my product and the nature of BLK/MRKT."

Like Fairey, Frank Kozik comes from a credible career as a poster artist and also works extensively with corporate clients. Noting the change over the ten years he's been doing corporate work, Kozik now has an uncharacteristic enthusiasm for a process he not long ago found stepped all over by heavy-handed art and creative direction. "I get paid a bunch of money, have my name on the product, and get to do whatever I want," Kozik relates. Branding beverages, producing his own line for Levi's, designing toys or creating campaigns for Altoids and Slim Jim, Kozik says "there's more latitude—as long as my ideas are manufacturable—I just have to worry about making things look cool. It's like they suddenly figured out 'if we just let these guys do what they want, we'll get better work for a lot less hassle.'"

Steve Powers, who has translated the street props of his graffiti career as ESPO into the markets of corporate and fine art commerce, recalls how "companies have come up with fucked-up preconceptions of what they wanted, which artists have had to respond to." ESPO was chosen by Calvin Klein, along with Futura and Delta, to co-brand

cK One perfume bottles with their own art. ESPO describes the experience, saying, "they were the first ones who left it all up to me. I know how to represent myself best, so if you just let me be me it's in everyone's best interest. That kind of change from such a high level sets a precedent, and Nike was like 'we want some of that medicine.'" Having been thrown in jail for graffiti, ESPO's commission for Nike's Blue Room house in Venice Beach used corporate sponsorship to turn the tables, as he, with full permission of the Los Angeles Mayor's office and Nike funding, went around LA covering up pre-existing graffiti in a style that mimicked the look of community-based graffiti erasure (known as "the buff") but discretely spelled out his own tag. Confessing that "I was lousy as a commercial artist when I tried, I had too much opinion," ESPO is one of many now discovering how the sudden glamour associated with art allows him a much more subtle and subversive interface with commerce. Director of Global Marketing for cK One, Lori Singer explains, "for us it starts with Calvin, who's seen this resurgence in graffiti and really challenged these artists to come up with their own personal interpretation and vision of the product. Art is a part of it, but it is also the trend of street culture in which graffiti marries well with the edginess and individuality of cK One."

One of a select few to make the move from the illegal graffiti movement to its brief but phenomenal moment in the art world zeitgeist of the early Eighties, Futura's prescience in walking away from the art establishment into the new media of co-branding in the early Nineties has made him a role model for younger artists pursuing this potent alternative. Enjoying some of the bigger co-branding opportunities (with cK One and Nike), Futura was an early figure in the artist toy and limited-edition sneaker product-genres and forged long relationships with the seminal players in this paradigm, including Agnès B. in France and Bathing Ape in Japan. Of the current climate, Futura says "what's happening in America right now is a bounce back from Japan. The point of sale has to be higher here, so every product has this huge financial risk, but there's just been so much noise generated out of Japan for their limited-edition artist projects that Western companies took notice."

Another pioneer to blaze the trail from the streets to the corridors of commerce that younger artists now access with the ease of a super-highway on-ramp is Haze. Working as an artist-designer for the record industry in the early years of Hip Hop and subsequently in the germinal eruption of street wear, Haze's art has more recently found less predictable canvas as a G Shock watch for Casio and a Fireblade motorcycle for Honda. "The Hip Hop underground was all about co-opting corporate culture," Haze remembers. "Artists riffing on corporate logos was a form of visual sampling. What happened was the people we were biting decided it was better to join us than to fight." That kind of ironic inversion of interests could be no better epitomized than by Kaws, who made his reputation with a fearless and formidable body of public work in which he painted over the ads on New York City bus stops. With Calvin Klein's sexed-up campaign always one of his favorite tar-

gets, Kaws now finds himself working on a project with them. "I've been painting over their stuff illegally for so long now, it's about time I got paid for it," he jokes. An equally ironic co-branding was afforded Belgian artist Wim Delvoye, creator of the infamous Cloaca machine (that mimics human digestion turning food into poop) exhibited at the New Museum. With an aesthetic fondness for corporate logos and a propensity for adapting them in his own art, Delvoye remembers "When Coca-Cola called me, I was worried they were coming after me for taking their logo." It turns out that, unaware of his previous unauthorized appropriations, "they were just looking to do something with contemporary art and asked me to put my art on their soda can."

Regarding the co-branding of today as "a renaissance of the artist as icon," Haze describes the moment at hand as "realizing you can become a part of corporate culture and take advantage of its multi-media infrastructure both in terms of visibility and economics without ultimately compromising your vision or integrity." Notions of compromise and integrity are hardly the sole province of the streets; they remain a paramount issue in the fine-art establishment—a bias that regards any transgression of its polite market elite as a degenerate form of commercialism. Karen Kimmel, an artist whose experience spans gallery exhibitions as well as creating K Bond, a high-end LA fashion store that carefully presented artist products as haute couture products, insists that "the gallery context is just as commercial, but under the pretext of art it gets very confusing. To be in a consumer-based medium today ultimately

"When Coca-Cola called me, I was worried they were coming after me for taking their logo. They were just looking to do something with contemporary art and asked me to put my art on their soda can."

Wim Delvoye

frees up an artist. You know what you're doing: making aesthetically pleasing products."

Donald Sultan, a mid-career artist firmly established in the six-figure range for his paintings, was recently approached by Neiman Marcus for use of his art. "I didn't want Neiman Marcus selling my fine-art prints in that context," he explains, "so I decided to create a limited-edition scent." Following an unlikely tradition of artist perfume co-brands that includes Marcel Duchamp and Andy Warhol, Sultan has created "Turpentine," to be sold at Neiman Marcus stores this year, along with a number of art-adapted products from cosmetic bags to scarves to playing cards. "There are a lot of things an artist can do that a designer can't," he explains. "You get to insert your imagery instead of having to adapt it. You don't have to make your art fit so much as find a way for everything else to fit around it." Of course, part of the attraction of co-branding for artists must also be the friction between high and low. When Takashi Murakami decided to work with Louis Vuitton, his New York gallerist Marion Boesky explains, "his art is about blurring, or even pushing aside, those boundaries between high and low. Like Duchamp and Warhol he is questioning what art is, but whereas they did it through appropriation he's actually collaborating with the 'enemy.' For Murakami, everyone should have access to art, especially those who are not necessarily cultured." Curious in this collaborative enterprise is that Murakami, who sold his art to Louis Vuitton, has decided to paint the same logos and imagery for his upcoming show at Boesky, and thus had to approach the company

for permission to paint his own art.

One significantly popular product venue for prominent contemporary artists over the past decade has been the ambitious edition of espresso cups by the Italian coffee company Illy. Begun in 1991 and including collaborations with Sandro Chia, Nam June Paik, David Byrne, Francis Ford Coppola and Jeff Koons, third-generation heir and corporate director Andrea Illy explains his collection: "The family mission since 1933 has been a concept of excellence to make the very best possible coffee. But we needed to get the goodness of the coffee attention in a culture that perceives it as a commodity. If you go back to Greek philosophy, goodness equals beauty. Beauty, the metaphysical condition of goodness, is only born in two places: nature and art." What started as a simple way to get attention has turned into a prestigious and lucrative line, with a major collector and re-sale base. Famous pop artist James Rosenquist, who not only did a cup with Illy but designed their logo, considers the process here as "like Madison Avenue—but it isn't." Regularly approached for other projects, such as one he was considering from a Spanish soccer team to design their jersey, Rosenquist flatly told us "it's great money of course, but at this point in my life I don't do just anything for money, my reputation is worth more than that."

For a sense of just how involved the dynamic between artists and corporate sponsorship is becoming, one needs only consider the many cultural artpreneurs who are moving into this nexus of convergent interests. Art critic Neville

■

■

Wakefield, who's landmark book on the impact of contemporary photographers on fashion photography, *Fashion,* (1994, Scalo) offers a prototype for the efforts of his new company, Sic, now suggests that "the operational metaphor of commerce is becoming as interesting as the white cube of the gallery." Carah Von Funk, who comes from a Hollywood film background and now operates Mama, precisely to mediate between artists and industry (including the recent Barnstormers project for H&M), explains that "many agencies have recently gone through a big down-sizing, so there's a lot of creative outsourcing for marketing, branding and advertising. We're just trying to help artists balance their financial and creative interests." For James Bond, proprietor of Undefeated, an LA store successfully filling the niche market of collectible limited-edition sneakers that runs an artist billboard project with Nike, it's a matter of "artists have been ripped off for so long, they finally just decided to get paid for it."

Forming Idealogue in 2000 with gallerist Bronwyn Keenan, fashion designer Jacqui Millar contends that "the old model of artists coming to fruition in the marketplace through a movement was a mono-culture that had the vile effect of rendering their energies impotent. We're in a new era, where artists need to think and negotiate as a network. For us, the paradigm shift is not to simply branding or endorsing something, but finding ways in which people can connect to one another, and how a corporation can be a medium for that." Idealogue's conceptual form of social branding, ranging from ambitious creative programs with Adidas to the recent redesign of

Soho fashion boutique Miss Sixty, is ultimately about investing in a kind of sustainable energy that can hopefully resist the passing fancy of consumer psychology, which may well relegate the use of fine artists to the dustbin of past trends. These kinds of stakes, of entrenching this discourse in a way that will avoid the built-in obsolescence of marketing desire to create a permanent matrix between creativity and product manufacture, are the very issues of survival now facing those few who first pioneered this uncommon ground.

Alife, a store on Orchard Street in New York's Lower East Side, has been on the early side (and perhaps short end) of the learning curve in exposing many of the artists now enjoying the current spate of aesthetic branding opportunities. Operating both as a quasi-gallery for artists to create retail-savvy installations and as a store specializing in artist-designed products, Alife recently made the full circle back to the art world collecting the greatest hits of their astute merchandising eye in a traveling exhibition (appropriately called Alife Store) that started at Deitch Gallery in New York and traveled to Robertson Tilton Gallery in Los Angeles. Co-founder Arnaud Delecolle recalls, "When we started, there was nobody pumping graffiti on the level we were. It was the last realm for kids to express themselves and talk to one another that was just for themselves and not about money." Collectively disheartened by the corporate feeding frenzy over many of the artists they helped launch and in particular, how their ideas have been so widely co-opted with no remuneration, co-founder Rob Cristofaro adds "as other stores are copying us, and everybody and their mother is trying to use artists to sell stuff, you can see how tired and timed it is, using the same old artists each time." Using their deep connection to the street cultures of graffiti and skateboarding to stay ahead of the pack, Alife now has a subsidiary business, Alife Creative, dedicated to co-branding and merchandising so that rather than merely functioning as an underground farm system, they can reap some of the fiscal rewards. Young Kim, a new partner in Alife Creative who brings with him an extensive marketing background, explains the reality in harsher terms: "From a corporate standpoint, working with an artist makes good sense, not simply in terms of the credibility but the creativity. Instead of paying a big advertising firm huge amounts of money, they can give an artist chump change to do a better job."

If anyone deserves the last word in this, it's certainly Aaron Rose, who's Alleged Gallery—first in New York and later in Los Angeles—helped launch the careers of so many at the front of the co-branding paradigm. With many artists now finding their way into the gallery system through the back door of corporate exposure, Rose found that the constant financial crisis of running a gallery was diminishing his more lucrative interests outside the proverbial white cube of the art market. Closing Alleged and forming Iconoclast with partner Christian Strike in 2002, Rose is now curating the Nike billboard project at Undefeated, producing a year-long magazine insert art-fanzine for Tylenol called *Ouch*, and co-curating a major museum show that will define this very moment at hand, "Beautiful Losers,"

to open at Cincinnati Art Center in Spring 2004. Understanding the situation from both sides of the art and commerce divide, Rose explains "having produced their own fanzines, tee shirts, skateboards, videos and everything else from the very beginning, making commercial products is really nothing new for these artists. A couple of years ago, when a few companies realized it made more sense to go to the artists directly instead of trying to co-opt them, it created an unprecedented level of creative freedom. What they finally realized is that there is no way to market to the younger generations from the outside anymore; the kids are just too savvy. Now, instead of fighting the art world or having to deal with ad agencies, I can be hired simply for having a built-in radar that they don't. And the deal they're now offering is—'just do what you do, and make sure we're in there somewhere.'"

"I was able to use the resources of a corpora-tion to make a positive contribution to the culture of graffiti. Instead of NIKE just being associated with a graffiti writer, they got to be down for the cause."

ESPO

ESPO

Steve Powers (ESPO) is an artist who lives and works in New York City.

Community Service

I left art school at the end of my sophomore year thinking that I could learn on the job. Why paint a stupid design exercise for a grade when I could paint a hoagie shop for a few bucks? At the end of the day, I would learn as much hustling work and more since I had to deal with a client and not some teacher dying to snuff out my dreams. I embarked on this idiot mission to be a full-time muralist, and I found plenty of ridiculous experiences, enough to learn that my dreams were too tough to die.

In the winter, when mural gigs are few, I worked in a restaurant running food from the kitchen to the table. It wasn't a bad job, except I had to endure the verbal jousting of the chef, who tried to get on everyone's last nerve. I had fun with him, knowing his dumb Southern-boy routine was an act, that he was smart enough to run two restaurants and was about to open a third. We got to talk about art, and he wanted some murals painted at his new restaurant and what would I charge for something like that? I told him it would be about triple what I made in the restaurant, because while I was a bad runner, I was a good artist and that costs. He cursed and laughed and told me that Van Gogh never sold a painting and Michelangelo was always broke and was I better than they were? I said I know what I'm worth, and it's not my fault if Vincent and Michael had self-esteem issues. So he said he'd hire me and true to his word, he did.

There was a catch. There always is. He had a vision! He wanted the wall by the kitchen to show a Vietnam vet enduring some Viet Cong–induced

trauma, then coming home to the USA where he's spat on by hippies, and he drinks and does drugs until the disillusion drives him out to the country. The country would be depicted on the wall next to the dining room, with fields of tomatoes and corn under a bright blue sky. The vet would find salvation as a farmer, raising the crops and sending the harvest back to the city. The vegetables are a metaphor for rebirth, growth, and purity; the vet is saved; and the city people are once again connected to their rural roots. I should mention that the chef who was laying out this plan, I would soon learn too well, was completely loaded on Percosets.

So I get a deposit, work up a sketch, get another deposit, and start painting. The restaurant is due to open in a few weeks, and there's a rush of activity all day, every day. My painting time is restricted to the late night, which is fine. I get to blast my rap mix tapes and paint this bizarre mural, which of course, takes a long time to do. Every night the chef would drive up in his jeep, walk in, and yell some criticism at me. "What the hell you got tomatoes here for, they should be squash you idiot!" Then he'd stumble back to his jeep and peel out. He never remembered what he yelled at me the day before, so I always said ok and kept painting. The night I finished, he crashed his jeep into the building, stumbled in like nothing happened, assumed his critical stance, and then shrugged. He crawled into a booth and passed out. A second later, the maître d' from the chef's restaurant up the street drove up in a panic, knowing the boss was too faded to drive safely. He checked the chef's vitals and helped me push the jeep back into the street. Once the vehicle was parallel to the curb, we helped ourselves to the warm Rolling Rock in the back seat.

The next day I went to see the chef, who was hungover and ashamed, so I got the rest of my money without incident. The mural was terrible; I just couldn't articulate the pilled-out vision of a troubled chef. The punchline came a couple of months later when the chef was profiled in a local paper, and he spoke about closing the restaurant. He said people were scared of the mural, that it ruined his business. It was the most damage I ever committed as a graffiti writer, and I got paid. You know I was happy, I'm sure Vincent and Michael would be too.

Good Sponsorship:

I am a morally ambiguous person at best, so I've taken money from a wide variety of wack companies whose 1099s testify to my low, low standards. I'd be happy to relate the best examples of whoring I've done, but mentioning them now is like turning two tricks for the price of one. Instead, I'll digress and tell you the best, with two hard-learned rules that make for a good collusion of art and commerce:

Don't be a tool.
Do something worthwhile or don't bother.

The first means that you have to put your needs ahead of the company you are doing work for. If they want you to rip yourself off for an ad campaign, tell them they're better off getting an intern to bite your style. The second quickly follows the first in that if the company is ready to let you be yourself, deliver the goods effectively without any internal conflict. Make art, show your good side, invoice promptly. Repeat until tired.

Nike commissioned me to do a show in their corporate conference center in Venice Beach. There was a budget with no demands as to what was to be represented, so I put the money to good use and executed a project about the eradication of graffiti and the heavy prosecution of graffiti writers in Los Angeles. I made my case in a good way, by painting illegally throughout the city for a few weeks. I was able to use the resources of a corporation to make a positive contribution to the culture of graffiti. Instead of Nike just being associated with a graffiti writer, they got to be down for the cause. It was like I went and picked a fight, and Nike threw me a knife. Ok, a butter knife, but still…

I wrote the following mission statement to clarify my position and give Nike some words to work with. It's a good indication of the spot I put Nike in, and they were good sports about it. They allowed me to make art on my terms, understood its worth, threw me a party, and gave me shoes. That's a good gig. I can count the number of those I've had on two middle fingers.

Community Service:

Graffiti, in case anyone missed the point, is a

marking on a surface. Graffiti eradication is typically the application of paint over the marking on the surface. In terms of "damage," there is no evidence that one layer of paint is less destructive than the one beneath it. In the course of painting over graffiti, the eradicators create a unique marking of their own that writers call "buffmarks." Roll along the highways of LA and see thousands of buffmarks, each as visually compelling as the next and the last, each with a story to tell.

The story is this: One person wrote a name to show he was there. Another person was threatened enough by this declaration of existence that he painted over the name. The splotch of paint that covers the name becomes a tag in itself. It sits on the wall and testifies to the presence of two people. One person is a so-called criminal, one is a so-called activist, and both are equal in their need to be recognized. One person has fame but faces jail; one person gets support and accolades from the community but wants fame. The wall could care less about either of them; it just gets fatter with paint.

Community Service is a project that poses the questions: If graffiti is painted in a way that serves a community, is it wrong? And, why aren't activists that make more of a mess painting over graffiti than the graffiti itself considered criminals?

I volunteered to paint over graffiti around the city, using my own supplies, to exploit the hypocrisy that people who put down one layer of paint are hated while the people who put down the next

layer are celebrated. At the same time, my mission was to paint my name in a bold and subtle style around the city to demonstrate the effectiveness of getting over in a civic-minded way. The answer, I suspected from the start, was that the only thing more pointless than painting graffiti is painting over it.

Graffiti is far from pointless, though. It is an adventure that employs innovation and critical thinking skills all in one stylish line. Painting over it isn't pointless either; it creates business and opportunities for hundreds of people all over LA. There is an intense symbiotic relationship between the writers and the buffers, and at the end of the day, if everyone has done his job, one person has created a mark and another person has covered it. So it is pointless, except for the decimal point on the dollar amount that graffiti abatement generates for the economy. That point moves steadily to the right morning, noon and night.

I'd like to thank Tim Badalucco, Darla Vaughn, and Aaron Rose for their outstanding contributions to the *Community Service* project.

"An artist who is sponsored is pledging an allegiance to the brand. This relationship rules out certain liberties in terms of expressing opinions, attitudes and subject matter that could be perceived as negative. Everything is happy in brand land."

Jacqui Millar

Jacqui Millar

The Whole > The Sum of Its Parts

IDEALOGUE is a high-end reality machine imagined by Mark Bromhead and Jacqui Millar. IDEALOGUE operates from a showroom linked to Bronwyn Keenan Gallery, where they collectively run a cultural and digital initiative called Kinetic Federation. (idealoguedomaine@hotmail.com)

Public diplomacy is a euphemism for propaganda the same way that sponsorship can create a "politically correct" limitation that negates free critical thinking and expression from the artist who is sponsored.

Traditionally artists have created new concepts for new worlds by communicating moral and social issues that confront the viewer in a cognitive discord that creates dialog.

Corporations shapeshift with culture, simulating "lifestyle" without a commitment to the real. Officially "neutral" on all social and moral issues, the corporate objective is to not alienate any niche markets that could be potentially profitable.

An artist who is sponsored is pledging an allegiance to the brand. This relationship rules out certain liberties in terms of expressing opinions, attitudes and subject matter that could be perceived as negative. Everything is happy in brand land.

Sponsorship can create a monoculture of "brand identities." When an artist in a movement is sponsored, it has a viral effect, rendering that movement impotent over time. A progressive sponsorship/artist would adapt to this changing environment to evolve with a new networked structure that creates meaningful connections between people: exchanging information, access and experience to create massively multiplayer knowledge ecologies.

Culture is a networked consciousness. It would be interesting if a brand approached sponsorship as a "medium" to effect real change—stimulating the development of a "post-individual" creative person as a cultural-environmental problem solver.

Sponsorship that is sustainable to culture, modeled on the "gift economy," would empower corporations to stop producing and reproducing the "real" and start nurturing the "real"— to participate in an era of extraordinary integrity.

"The show thus takes a poke at the fine-art world's dependence on corporate support, but also asks whether sponsorship is evidence of good corporate citizenship, or merely a refined form of product placement."

Rob Walker

Rob Walker

Your Logo Goes Here

Rob Walker is a journalist living in New Orleans. He writes the Ad Report Card *column for* Slate *and has written about marketing and other subjects for* The New York Times, The New Republic, *and* The Boston Globe. *This essay originally appeared on Slate.com. (robwalker.net)*

Last month, when a small Los Angeles art gallery called BLK/MRKT opened its new show *Sponsorship*, a more-than-capacity crowd turned up. Hundreds of people (including, rumor has it, Keanu Reeves) were unable to get in before the fire marshal shut the proceedings down. Curiously, all this buzz was for an art exhibit with no art. The visuals are just logos, chosen not for aesthetic reasons, but for monetary ones: the inclusion and display size of the logos was a matter of who agreed to sponsor the show and how much they paid.

Solicitations went out last summer (2002) to hundreds of companies who were told they could get into the show at various sponsorship levels according to how much they were willing to pony up in cash, services, and merchandise ($500 earned "Patron of the Arts" status; $1,000 got "Bronze Medallion Status," and so on). Many of the companies who chose to play along were niche-oriented shoe or skateboard firms and the like. The bigger names included Levi's, AOL, Yahoo!, Kinko's, and Red Bull.

Sponsorship aims to make an interesting point or two about the intersection of art and commerce. These days we're all used to seeing corporate names and logos lurking on museum walls just a few feet from art works. Corporate sponsorship of fine art and cultural events became gradually more widespread from the *1960*s and was basically a given by 1985, when the director of New York's Metropolitan Museum of Art commented to the New York Times, "There is no question that because we have become dependent on corporate

sponsorship, we keep an eye on which shows are likely to be funded by corporations and which are not."

So, the motivation for the art world to gin up sponsors is obvious. But what exactly are the corporations in it for? Sometimes the patronage payoff is pretty obvious. Dior once sponsored a Met exhibition on Christian Dior, and Tiffany sponsored a Met Tiffany show. Another Met exhibition, *The Man and the Horse*, relied on a grant from Ralph Lauren of Polo fame. Mobil (now part of ExxonMobil) sponsored exhibitions of art from Cameroon, Nigeria, and other "countries we do business with," a spokeswoman for that company once explained.

In other instances, the link is not as direct but is still easy to suss out. Philip Morris has been a patron of modern art since at least 1965, when it underwrote a Pop and Op Art show. In her 1999 book No Logo, Naomi Klein quoted a brand manager explaining that Tequiza had backed a "risqué" George Holz show because "art was a natural synergy with our product." This was an example, to Klein, of firms "thirstily soaking up cultural ideas and iconography that their brands could reflect by projecting these ideas and images back on the culture as 'extensions' of their brands."

What *Sponsorship* does so cleverly is simply remove culture from the equation. There's no brand extension here for the "patrons" to exploit; it's just them. The show thus takes a poke at the fine-art world's dependence on corporate support, but also asks whether sponsorship is evidence of good corporate citizenship, or merely a refined form of product placement. A release about the show takes a line similar to Naomi Klein's, saying that the show and its forthcoming catalog examine how "companies that want to appear 'down' with a certain demographic have attempted to co-opt an honest, organic, and real culture with a commercial one."

But the real message is actually a little more subtle than that. *Sponsorship* was shown in BLK/MRKT Gallery. In addition to being a gallery space, it is the design studio of Shepard Fairey, who is probably best known for the famous *Obey Giant* sticker-and-stencil phenomenon familiar to urbanites all over the country, if not the world. Neither McGinness nor Fairey, then, is interested in blanket condemnation of commerce; instead they seem interested in provoking their audience to see that the lines between art and capital are blurry everywhere you look.

Some of the better-known participants are actually clients of BLK/MRKT. One major participant who bought in solely on the basis of a cold call was Scion, the new Gen Y–targeted car from Toyota. "Scion is branding by as many noncorporate methods as possible," explains Jeri Yoshizu, a Scion promotions manager. Major concert tours and sporting events are out for now, in favor of "communities and businesses and causes that are relevant to the core Scion segment." So, depending on how you look at that statement, Scion was pumping its brand among the below-the-radar and ahead-of-the-curve market

leaders—or trying to appear "down" with a certain demographic. Or—and of course this is the correct answer—both.

Yoshizu's only complaint was that the company's logo in the show identified the car as the "Toyota Scion," rather than simply "Scion." "Other than that," she adds, "I thought it was super cool. I did feel that we were being mocked, but what the hell."

Interviews

"I feel like everybody's on this bullshit art tip. Everybody wants a piece of it. It's crazy just seeing it in the past three, four years. All these companies want to associate everything with an artist now, no matter what they do."

Tony Arcabascio (SITE)

Tony Arcabascio

Tony Arcabascio (SITE): Queens, Long Island, BMX, graffiti, break dance, smoke, fuck, fight, night clubs, St. John's University, BMW, tee design, vampires, Jen, "what's your god?" campaign, Alife NYC, Brooklyn, paint clothes, Alife Rivington Club, Alife Creative, rock 'n' fuckin' roll, god?

RM: So, Tony, we've talked about this whole situation before, but now I want to get your opinion on what's going on from your point of view within Alife.

TA: I have a fucked-up view on this whole shit, but I almost can't say what I really think. Sometimes I feel like, get the fucking money and fuck being cool. With me, it's what are my own partners going to say, that's like my family. That's how I consider the people that I work with, and sometimes we don't agree.

RM: You all have to all agree before you decide to take on a project? Does it have to be unanimous?

TA: It's got to be unanimous, and a lot of times we don't do projects individually, because it's not agreed upon within the whole group. We sort-of got it to the point where everything we do goes through the company, whether we do it individually or not.

RM: What does that mean? You did the Levi's thing under your own name...

TA: I did it under my own name. Alife was involved in credits and things. It still said "Alife," but as far as money goes...

RM: Do you use your individual names?

TA: That's it; everything we do. Yeah, like with that denim book we just did. It's "Tony and Alife."

RM: So that there is a sort of co-branding.

TA: Yeah, that's true. What's cool is that we got, the four of us, we all got different fucking styles, now we just took on Young, who is in the creative section of our company, and he's got a whole other style. It's like subdivisions of this thing. So it's cool; and it's not even a matter of us not wanting to do it for Alife, because I love putting that

after my name. To me, that strengthens the whole shit. That's my crew, you know. I'm proud of them. I go around sticking up whatever stickers, and I'm sticking up Alife stickers simultaneously.

RM: What about Alife working for another company? What are some of the projects that you've done?

TA: We just did three Adidas/Alife NYC pairs of sneakers for our new clothing line. It was great. We were working with Abby Guyer. She's the coolest chick in the world. We've always had a relationship with Adidas, because of the sneaker store, so it was just something that came up. I think we actually asked them, but they automatically jumped on it, and it was a perfect marriage. We have, not to be a dick, one of the best sneaker stores in the world.

RM: Why work with Adidas for this particular project? What can they do for you? Distribution?

TA: No, because we're not really letting them do that. It's a pretty small run. They have great quality shit, so it's like they have great silhouettes already. We took pre-existing styles, and we just tweaked the fabrics and added special stuff from regular leather to kangaroo. So it's little things like that and colorways and all that stuff to create a brand new shoe. We mixed a couple elements of one shoe and brought it into another shoe, but the body shapes were basically there. We did three styles: we did the Grand Slam, the Attitude, and the Top Cut.

RM: As far as the branding goes on the shoe itself, how does that go?

TA: It's an Adidas sneaker with "Alife NYC" right on the side of the shoe.

RM: Have you had other companies approach

you that you've had to turn down?

TA: We try to think of ourselves as the best at what we do, or we try to be the best at what we do. So, we want to join up with the best. Sometimes that doesn't match with another company who doesn't have the same aesthetic as us, or they don't have the same beliefs, or we don't think they're going in the same direction as us. We try to think of the future, like what this brand is going to be in a couple of years. Is that who we want to fuck with right now, and what happens if they turn, or they start pumping mad shit out? So, we've always got to look ahead, and I think that's how we decide who we want to fuck with. We plan on being around, and we're not going to screw it up now for later.

RM: How does it break down?

TA: We've got the Alife retail store. The first one is on Orchid Street, and then we have the Alife Rivington Club, which is our sneaker shop. We have the men's line, "Alife NYC;" the women's line, "Uptown Tammy;" and a sneaker line called "Rite Foot." Most recently, we have the traveling store/installation that actually sells shit. Everybody jumped on the bandwagon of doing the gallery in the store, so we decided to flip it—to do a store in a gallery.

RM: Do you see getting to the point where you would be a Footlocker in Mall of America, operate on that kind of level?

TA: I don't think we'll ever make Alife into something where you have ten in one city, but I'll be honest with you, I wouldn't mind having one in each major city. I could see that happening, and it probably will.

RM: Talk about the Truth and Levi's campaigns.

TA: Levi's I love, so it was a no-brainer for me. I wear Levi's. That's what I've worn for a long time. I wear other denim brands also, but that's definitely one of my favorites.

RM: They approached you on this?

TA: Yeah, well, actually they were looking for artists, and Alife submitted a bunch of artists, and out of ten that we threw at them they picked three out of our group. It was easy, and that's one of the reasons why I wanted to do it.

RM: They came to you and said, "Will you paint on this denim, and we'll use it as artwork in the campaign?"

TA: Yeah. I didn't know exactly how it was going to end up. But it was definitely for their ad campaigns and for their own personal archive. They actually have two pairs of jeans that I painted for them. They get to keep them for two or three years and then I either get them back if I want them, or they have to auction them off.

RM: How are you going to keep track of that?

TA: You just reminded me. I've got to call them.

RM: In this Levi's thing, was it a situation like "Tony for Levis?"

TA: Yeah, they used my name. They credited all the artists on a poster, and Alife was involved. Levi's did this whole bio thing where they sent the booklet out to people.

RM: Was that a selling point for you? Exposure?

TA: It spread the word about Alife. It was pretty early in our history. We were only in business for a year and a half, so it was a cool opportunity to work with a good company that I believed in, and it worked out fine. I actually got more out of it than I expected. They opened up a new store here and I got to paint stuff at their store. I thought it was just a cool thing to do. It was actually one of my first real projects with a company like that, and I thought it was exciting. I got a little bit of play off it, and it was a cool experience.

RM: What was that other project you did around the same time? The Truth campaign?

TA: There were three artists in three locations. It was me, ESPO and Kinsey. Kinsey painted a wall, I painted a wall, and ESPO painted a truck. It was basically for the anti-smoking campaign which was a little funny, because I'm such a fucking smoker.

RM: How did that come about?

TA: The photographer knew of a bunch of us, and had been working with us. She wanted to show some of our shit. So, again, like with Levi's, we gave her a couple of different artists' shit, and they liked my stuff. So, I banged out a wall in a day.

RM: Why did you decide to do it?

TA: At that point I just wanted to do a wall. I hadn't done a wall in a while, and it was legal, and it was easy, and I was fucking around with some new design shit—a new aesthetic, and I wanted to see how it would transcribe to a wall. I had never done a wall in this new style, so I tried it out and it came out pretty well. It was just a way for me to do something and get something out of it.

RM: And get paid for it?

TA: Exactly. It was pretty easy. I banged it out in one fucking day.

RM: Were there any terms to negotiate?

TA: No, it was pretty easy. I think that's what I enjoy about doing jobs. If it's easy, and it flows nice, and I don't have to worry about it…like I

knew the photographer already. I knew she wasn't going to fuck around. It was pretty easy flowing and they sent some nice guys to assist me and help out and whatever. It was just easy. If you know you can do it and get it done in a couple of days, and it's done, and you get paid, and it's over, then anything after that is gravy. If it comes out in a magazine, then yo, yeah. If they decide to make a commercial, then alright.

RM: On that note, what if they do more than you bargained for?

TA: Oh yeah, there was all that in my contract. Also, they were supposed to make a commercial out of it, but I think in the end they didn't. I think it didn't happen, because there was a stencil thing being done, and they were afraid kids were going to get the wrong idea and go out and start painting shit.

RM: And I remember you telling me how you were smoking as you were painting.

TA: I would forget, because automatically I'd be painting, and I'd just light up, and all of a sudden they'd ask me a question. I'd turn around and they would be like, "Cut!" So, it's pretty funny. They'd ask, "Is that a cigarette in his mouth?"

RM: All these situations seem pretty straight forward and casual.

TA: We can't fuck with people who are going to bring some big ordeal. We know what we want to do. So, if we know what we want, and you know what we want, then it should be easy.

RM: Have there ever been any bad experiences?

TA: I really can't think of that many off hand, because we've pretty much kept to ourselves. We've always built up our own brand. That's all we've really focused on in the past fuckin' three-

and-a-half to four years. We're coming up on four years now, and it's like we never really had to worry about anybody outside. The only outside people we had to worry about were people trying to bite our shit, or coming in and trying to fuck with us. Now we're seeing some problems, but not with big companies—more like production things, because we're starting to grow.

RM: Do you ever change your opinion about an artist or their work because of a project that they've done with a company?

TA: Everybody has their opinions. Sometimes you see something, and you think, "How the fuck did this happen?" and then you realize, "Oh, it's probably the fucking money. These motherfuckers must have gotten paid to do this shit, otherwise why would they do it?" I feel like everybody's on this bullshit art tip. Everybody wants a piece of it. It's crazy just seeing it in the past three, four years. All these companies want to associate everything with an artist now, no matter what they do. Everybody wants to do something with this art scene that's happening now, which is a great thing. It's cool, but I feel like everybody's worried about how they're going to look. I contradict myself, because I know I say to myself like, "Fuck it man. Get paid, because you don't know how long this shit's going to last. How long is this up-the-artists-ass movement going to go on?" Then there's a part of me that says, "But you look like a dick if you do it," you know? There are some days when I get so frustrated.

RM: What's up with that denim book you just did? Did you experience this same conflict?

TA: That was with Cone Mills. They make denim for a lot of companies. It was mostly a trade pub-

lication that's more for the industry. It's not supposed to be sold in retail stores, and I don't think it is, but I know someone told me the last one was sold at St. Mark's Bookstore. This is a project where they went to the publisher of Nylon Magazine, and he came to me. He said that he had this two-book deal that he had to do for Cone, and he had another guy art direct the last one. I said the only way I would fuck with this is if I could creative direct. I have certain ideas that I want to portray in the stories, and I told him that I wasn't going to use models, and I wasn't going to use stylists. And since he has a rock and roll background too, I thought he'd definitely go for the idea of me giving it a rock twist. There wasn't really any money in it, but I thought it was the right time. I wanted to get it out, because I had plans for a bigger project—the record cover project that I'm working on right now, which is going to be out this summer.

RM: How are you funding that?

TA: I'm actually hooked up with a friend of ours, Alex from Neverstop. I think it was a great marriage, because his company publishes books, and they press vinyl. Also, he has distribution which is pretty similar to ours, so it was a perfect match. Like I said, I like to keep my shit stress-free, and working with Alex, who is a friend, I knew it would be stress-free. He sees the same way I see, and he lets me do what I do. That's the one thing I think is cool about this whole period—a lot of people who are similarly minded are starting their own companies, so we don't need these bigger companies. The money's not all there, but we're all doing our own shit now. I've got one friend who's a printer; I've got another friend who's got a record label, and I don't need to go to anybody else. I can just call up my friends. I don't have to worry about going through the secretary or dealing with this guy or dealing with their lawyers or any bullshit.

RM: But what about the companies that are always trying to reach into Alife?

TA: They're going to take it anyway—whether you work with them or not. They're going to take it, and if you don't want to fucking do it, you don't want to do it, they'll go get someone else. Do you join them and get paid, or don't join them and let them fucking bite your shit? You're going to be frustrated either way, but at least if you do it, you got a little money. That's something we face every day. Those companies have people who come in here, buy shit without even trying anything on. They drop a thousand dollars, and they didn't try one motherfucking thing on. In two weeks they can have that shit knocked off, produced, and in the store. It's an incredible thing. We had a scarf in here that was done by a small designer. Someone came in and bought it, and two-and-a-half weeks later, a guy came in here with the same scarf on but instead of one star it had two. There's nothing you can do. I have friends who work at these big fashion companies and put together these "inspiration boards." My friends are like, "Tone, you'll never believe it. I went into a meeting today, and your shit was on this thing…" What are you going to do? That's the cycle. That's why we're here, I guess—so people can take from us.

RM: Is it possible to take back?

TA: No, unless you've got money. You need money to take back. If someone's got more money than you, that's it. They're going to take. What you can take and how much you can take from people depends on how much money you have. Look what happened to us with Vans.

RM: Now that's a great story. Can you elaborate?

TA: It's over, and I don't even like to talk about it. It's been this two-year battle, but basically we did a slip-on shoe for Alife Rite Foot. A slip-on is a slip-on. It's been done since the beginning of time. Vans got it from Keds, and we put a pattern on ours,—an argyle pattern. Vans was saying that their little checkerboard pattern was the same as our big-ass argyle pattern. Now to me, they've got two different names, because they're two different fucking things: one's a checkerboard and one's an argyle. Otherwise, they'd both be fucking called checkered. They made ridiculous demands, and basically their only reason for coming after us was because they wanted to put us out of business. They dragged out this court case for two years. It cost us hundreds of thousands of dollars to battle this shit. For what? They didn't even offer us a cease and desist—straight to court. That's unheard of. They thought we were going to cave. They thought we were going to give in, and we fought that shit, and we worked our asses off to make the money to pay for that shit. We had good fucking lawyers, and that's why it cost so much. Vans fucking backed down in the end, because they saw it wasn't working. We're so down with fucking skating and BMX-ing—that's my whole life. I wore Vans. Half our staff are pro or semipro, and it didn't make sense to me. Maybe we're more than what we think we are. Vans has to come fuck with us, and that makes us feel good in a way. These motherfuckers felt so threatened that they had to come after us.

RM: In your space you host exhibitions and work with artists in a way that's different than other "cross-platform spaces." With each exhibition, you produce a product with the artist. Why do you think that works so well at Alife?

TA: Because we're not abusive. We don't make fucking money off that shit. That's not why we do it, so money's not even a factor. The reason that we do the product is so that it extends the exhibition. If we can help the artists grow, then that's a step for all of us. They can leave here and go do a bigger show somewhere else. That's only going to help us. What is that artist going to say when he gets press? "I had my first show at Alife." That's cool. That's all we want. That's one of the reasons we did that Deitch thing. That shit doesn't really make money. That was a way for us to pump all our friends' stuff. We consider all these guys our friends. That's one of the criteria for people that we work with. You could have the coolest shit in the world, but if you're a dick, I ain't putting your shit in the store.

RM: I assume the same holds true for the clothing labels you put in the store and the companies you choose to work with.

TA: Exactly, but we're careful. All these companies are tying to get their cred back. They're trying to get their cool factor back, and they see the money is in this youth market. Who will they sponsor next? How much longer is this going to last? It makes me think that maybe you should get paid now. Maybe you should be taking all these fucking jobs with all these big companies and get fucking cashed out, because maybe in fucking five years, they'll be sponsoring fucking policemen or firemen. The blue-collar worker could be the next fucking thing. Who knows what the next shit is going to be? Living in New York costs a lot of fucking money. A lot of these cats come from nothing, and if someone approaches them with a couple of bucks, and they know they can live for the next two, three months, that's pretty much a no-brainer. It's hard to blame the artist sometimes.

Craig Costello

Craig Costello (KR) lives and works in and around lower Manhattan. Graffiti, photography, painting and product development are main points of interest. He has his own homemade ink and markers called Krink. His work has been in various publications and shown in all kinds of places. (krink.com)

RM: What corporate-sponsored projects have you been involved in and why?

KR: I haven't been in many corporate-sponsored events. I did a billboard for Nike, which I think applies to your project. I did graffiti-style handwriting for them. Basically, it was their words and my writing. They included my name next to the Nike logo. Why? For the money and the spot.

RM: May I ask you how much they paid you?

KR: $1,000.00

RM: What did you think about them including your name next to the swoosh? Do you think that kind of thing benefits you or them more?

KR: I was glad that they included my name next to theirs. They could have easily gotten anybody to do the job. Since Nike put my name on the billboard, I got the exposure in a good spot, Fordham Road in the Bronx. A lot of people saw it in the Bronx, and I don't have anything else up there. So for me, it was good. As for them, who knows? It was a flash in the pan.

RM: Do you consider what you did for them to be your art, or simply a work-for-hire job?

KR: Work. It was their concept and their copy. I just wrote what they wanted.

RM: What corporate-sponsored projects have you rejected and why?

KR: I was asked if I wanted to redesign or paint a shoe or something so the organizers could get some Nike money for a show. At the time, I didn't absolutely need Nike to make it happen, and I thought that a lot of the sponsored projects I had seen where cheesy. I didn't want to be a part of that.

RM: When you say that you didn't need Nike to make it happen, was that because you didn't need

the money, or because you didn't see any merit in the project?

KR: I didn't want Nike all up in my shit. I had a show in a space and it was all working fine and on time. To throw a Nike shoe into the mix was unappealing to me.

RM: Can I ask you to elaborate on what makes a project cheesy?

KR: I've been to events, parties, whatever, where the artists are just window dressing for an office party. There is no money for the artist. The artist is just hoping to get exposure or to make contacts and participate. There are so many projects where a company is like "Let's get these artists to redesign a shoe, shirt, pants, or whatever." For the artist, all to often, there's no money. As you know, it costs money and time to produce most artwork. I think if the corporation really cared, they would give more attention to the artwork. When you're really big willy, you get Gucci to sponsor your event and have them drop lots of cash on your project. Look at Richard Serra— ain't nothing wrong with that. When you're a newjack, you have to jump through hoops and take handouts. That's just the way it is.

RM: What are the motives for both artists and corporations to work together?

KR: For the artist, money and exposure: living and helping in the manufacturing of a piece. I would say it really comes down to money and exposure. For a corporation, supporting art and artists as well as positioning in a certain demographic and audience.

RM: I'd like to zero in on exactly these two issues: money and exposure. There must be some boundaries and thresholds for both. Every case

"When you're really big willy, you get Gucci to sponsor your event and have them drop lots of cash on your project. When you're a newjack, you have to jump through hoops and take handouts. That's just the way it is."

Craig Costello (KR)

is different, but can you give me some rule of thumb for what amount of each you seek? For example, are the two inversely proportional to one other? Does a good amount of money counterbalance an undesirable or limited audience? And vice versa?

KR: I would like all the money and all the exposure I can get. If I were offered a lot of money to do something that I didn't really like, I would do it for the dough, unless I thought it was really bad or ripping someone else off. It would be nice if it were something that I could get behind, but you can't always choose. There is work and getting paid for a job, and then there is art that you are going to do no matter what. As far as exposure, I need all the exposure I can get. If it was like "OK, KR, let's take your art and use it to sell our product," I hope I would get paid a bundle. I'd rather have a company sponsor a show or piece than do an ad campaign for them.

RM: And as far as exposure goes, are you looking to get up in front of just anyone with pure numbers being the goal, or are you concerned with the quality of your audience? I suppose this is a question of quality vs. quantity.

KR: The quality of audience? I don't want to be too stuffy. I love contemporary art, and I'm also a graffiti writer. Art can be high-minded and a little exclusive sometimes. That's fine, but I also want everyday people to experience and enjoy art. I would prefer if everyone had a chance to experience and appreciate artwork.

RM: Concerning KRINK, have you ever been approached by a company about producing or distributing it?

KR: Not by a big company. Given its history, I think Krink is still a little too edgy for a really big company to be involved.

RM: Let's assume a company were interested. What would you look for in that kind of a relationship?

KR: Production, distribution, product development. Often times, when a big company buys into a little company, the smaller company can benefit from the larger infrastructure (buying power). If a large company were interested in Krink, and that company could provide the things I listed, I think it might be worth it for me.

"I have definitely talked to fools on the phone who don't even know my name, and they're like, 'Derek, we have this project we think you'd be hot for.' Now that's a red flag in my book."

DALEK

DALEK

James Marshall (DALEK) received a BFA from the
Art Institute of Chicago in 1995. He has worked
for Takashi Murakami, studied art and biology, and
exhibited widely. He lives and works in Brooklyn.
Nickel-Plated Angel, a collection of his work, is
being published by Gingko Press. (dalekart.com)

RM: What corporate-sponsored projects have you
been involved in?

DALEK: I've been involved with a few corporate-
sponsored events. With Nike, I did an ad for their
Presto shoe line that ran in NYC during the summer of 2002. The campaign covered bus shelters,
phone booths, and subway stations.

RM: What was the exact deal with that? Nike
asked a bunch of artists to create new work or did
they license existing work? How much money was
involved?

DALEK: They asked 6 artists, I believe, to create
new artwork for an outdoor print campaign in
New York for their Presto shoe line. The money
involved was millions of pennies—not as much
as people would like to believe. I sell out cheap.
All I really wanted was a jogging suit so I could
look fresh.

RM: Looking fresh is important. I know for
myself, when I think I look fresh, it boosts my
self-confidence, and I can often do things I
wouldn't have the nerve to do otherwise. I'm sure
Nike, by the same token, wanted to look fresh
to boost the public's confidence in Presto and
therefore asked you to create work for them.
Did they trust you completely to do your thing,
or did they set parameters?

DALEK: They gave me only one parameter for
the project, which was to have "movement":
simulated motion.

RM: Perhaps you should have given THEM
parameters! "You can only use my work in such-n-
such a way and only for so long, etc." Do you feel
like you weren't in a position to do so and that
Nike held presentation power over your work?

DALEK: No, it was actually already handled like

that. It was a 1-year usage fee, strictly for outdoor
use, strictly U.S. I still maintained all rights to the
artwork. So there were no issues in that vein.

RM: And the Nike logo?

DALEK: The Nike and Presto logos on the ads
were minimal and didn't interfere at all with the
artwork. Now that's alright. Obviously, if they had
asked me to draw a character wearing Nikes and
shouting out Nike and things of that nature, it
might have been a different story.

RM: You're defining a line between a company
sharing the same real estate as your work (the logo
existing within the same picture plane) and
product placement within your narrative. Is this
accurate?

DALEK: Basically what I'm saying is that I
didn't have to compromise the artwork. I wouldn't
normally draw a character wearing Nike shoes, so
it would be a little awkward for me to have to do
something like that. Or if there had been a big
Nike shoe with a space monkey sticking out of it
or sliding down it—that's the difference. If the
Nike logo had been 10 times larger than the
characters, that might have sucked. I don't know.

RM: So the issue comes down to whether or not
you feel like you're compromising your work and
if you're being asked to create something you
wouldn't normally create had Nike not been paying you. Is there a threshold for doing that kind
of work-for-hire? How much would it have cost
Nike to get your space monkey to wear their
shoes?

DALEK: That's a good question. I'd like to think
that there is a point where the answer would be
an emphatic "No!", but circumstances might arise
in which I'm sure it could happen, and there is

definitely a way I could justify it to myself if need be. It would really have to be in my face to know what I would do for sure. It might depend on how empty my bank account is at that particular moment. Money isn't the be-all end-all in life, but I'd be lying if I said I didn't want any.

RM: This is what seems to haunt a lot of us. Beyond the need to share the work and reach more people, we all need to provide ourselves (and families) with at least the basics. Have you ever considered making money in an entirely different field from art so as to clearly separate the two pursuits? This seems to have been the approach artists of previous generations took.

DALEK: I have had "day jobs" while pursuing and working on art. The problem with that, for me, becomes time and energy. I have to be in a certain mindset to draw and paint, and I don't know if I could fulfill the potential of pursuing art while holding down a 9 to 5. If I worked all day and then had to come home and paint all night and on the weekends, I would be denying my wife the time and attention she deserves. I like being able to work on my art all day and kind of seeing where it goes. Granted, there are times, such as right now, when I'm broke and there isn't anything in the immediate future that looks to resolve that. I believe in what I am doing, though, and feel that I need to stick to it 100% until I absolutely have no choice. But even in this situation, I wouldn't take on a project that I don't feel right about, regardless of the money. One thing that I think can subsidize the art, and is considered by many to be art, is the sale of commercial products—prints, books, shirts, toys, placemats, etc. This is an interesting topic in and

of itself. Just look at the Alife shop in the Deitch gallery.

RM: That's right. I think someone once said, "Products are the new art." What's another example of a sponsored project you've been involved in?

DALEK: In the summer of 2002, I participated in a show in London that was sponsored by the shoe company Royal Elastics.

RM: Of course. We were in that show together, and the best part of that trip was hanging out with you, Shepard, and Rich in the pubs. I remember finding out upon arrival at the gallery that Royal Elastics actually paid the rent for the gallery or gave them money for hosting the show. And there was a Royal Elastics shoe box on display in the gallery, etc. What was your response to all that?

DALEK: Hanging out definitely made it all worthwhile. That was good fun, indeed. I certainly felt cheated when I found out the gallery had been rented. It was like the gallery could care less about the show. They just got their rent paid in the downtime of summer. I mean, they were great guys, and no ill will to them, but there was a lot of weirdness. The ads placed in the catalogs for the show were color coordinated to the artist's work that it interrupted—not really cool. The shoe box shit was the bottom end. What's the point of hanging a shoe box in the gallery? I mean, great, you sponsored the show, and you flew us to England. I am grateful for that, but it's an art show. Like I said, live and learn. I think the project was too big and too overwhelming for those putting it together, and the art got lost in the mix of media frenzy and press lunches.

RM: Yeah, I think a lot of the artists felt weird about that show as the situation unfolded.

DALEK: That show is a good example of something that wasn't ideal. In that case, I feel the sponsorship interfered with the art and was problematic. Sometimes you may not know until it's too late. Which was the case there. Live and learn.

RM: Tell me about your BLK/MRKT show.

DALEK: In November I did a show at the BLK/MRKT gallery in Los Angeles for which 55DSL paid to have a print made for the show. They were therefore a sponsor of the show. Red Bull was also a sponsor of that particular show.

RM: That's right. Is there a 55DSL logo on the print? Why do you think 55DSL would pay for the production of your prints?

DALEK: Because they like us. I figure it's because they want to be associated with that scene —young, urban, and image savvy. I mean, they are young too, and that is what they are into. They were nice folks. I ain't mad at them. It's all good.

RM: But to put their logo on your print? Does that compromise the integrity of your work?

DALEK: The integrity issues for me are whether or not I like a company and what they do, how they plan on using the artwork, and if there is artistic freedom within the project. With Nike, for example, it was a great experience. I am a fan of Nike. I own many Nike products, and they were easy to work with.

RM: In liking Nike, is it the company you are responding to, or their brand?

DALEK: What I like about the company is the quarterly reports. I find their accounting department to be one of the top in the world, with an estimated annual growth of 2.66179%. And that swoosh is cool. It's just like the Newport cigs logo flipped. That's hot. What I like about Nike is the brand. Sure, since I was a kid I've worn Nikes. The first Air Jordans were all I wore when they came out. I want to be like Mike, too. I go to Nike Town all the time and buy shitloads of stuff.

RM: I really want to press this issue. When you were younger, you may have been naïve to the inner workings of a company like Nike and only interested in Nike's brand image. However, now that you are older and a more mature consumer, that may not be the case anymore. A lot of people would argue that Nike is a big evil company that supports sweatshops with inhumane working conditions in Indonesia and contributes to the globalization of a bland monoculture. So, I'm curious if a company's politics enter the picture when deciding to work with them.

DALEK: I don't get involved in politics. Maybe someday I will. As far as globalization of a bland monoculture goes, I don't buy into it. Starbucks, McDonalds, Coca-Cola…what have you…I don't see them dissolving the fabric of culture. Maybe they are. God bless their tiny little souls. I enjoy many products created and/or sold by mega-corporations. I ain't angry at them. If a company's politics conflicted with mine, obviously I would not work with them. I know what Nike does, or what I hear Nike does. I understand people don't like Nike. I am sure there are plenty of reasons not to. I can't even get into that. I'll be sleeping in my Nike basketball shorts tonight.

RM: So the motives are…

DALEK: The motives are money—for everyone involved. Obviously I would like to pay my rent and such things. And the corporations are looking to identify themselves with what is going on and find new audiences for their products. Corporations have sponsored art for ages. Go to any major corporation and look around. There are paintings and sculptures everywhere.

RM: I think there's a big difference between corporate art collections (where companies will buy the pre-existing work of an artist as a means of diverting profits and making investments—or perhaps as selfless acts of pure patronage!) and corporations doing either of the following: sponsoring art projects in exchange for credit or creating limited-edition product art that co-brands the corporation with the artist.

DALEK: You're right. There is a difference. I shouldn't try to get all intellectual at 8 in the morning. Pull my card motherfucker. It's all good. Obviously every person has his or her opinions on the right and wrong of it. Working with corporations for me…I use my judgment the best I can to accept or decline projects of such a nature.

RM: Every case is going to be different. What I'm trying to do is provide both sides with some insight into what the other is thinking. So for you personally, are there any more rules of thumb you use in making your decisions?

DALEK: It's usually just a gut thing. Nine times out of ten it pays off. I usually know right out of the gate whether or not something feels right. I'm sure you know.

RM: Your intuition plays a huge role in making those kinds of decisions?

DALEK: A lot of it depends on the company— their approach and ideas for a particular project. You can usually tell if someone is really into what

you are doing and in tune with what is going on, or if you're just a buzz word floating across their desk. If a company has a good reputation, and history for creating good projects, then it's all good. The contact people are a big part of it. Like dealing with any individual—sometimes there is a chemistry, and you know it's going to work. I have definitely talked to fools on the phone who don't even know my name, and they're like, "Derek, we have this project we think you'd be hot for." Now that's a red flag in my book.

RM: Ha! So, Derek, someone told me you're hot hot hot right now. Can you design a line of t-shirts for us that has your astro monkey thingy smoking our brand of cigarettes?

DALEK: Only if the check has as many zeros as the smoke ring I'm blowing out my ass right now…and if I can have a few packs for my kids.

RM: Is there any separation you feel you've had to make among your various pursuits? Can you address the use of the name "Dalek" as opposed to using your real name?

DALEK: Using the name "Dalek" for me is just a simple identifier. It is easier for people to hum, if you will. "James Marshall" is a great name, don't get me wrong. I enjoy it, but "Dalek" seems more natural to me for these pursuits.

RM: Can you give me an example (in addition to the "Derek" one) of a project you felt wasn't a good match for you?

DALEK: This project I did for Levi's a couple years back through Houston Gallery in Seattle. They wanted a very specific kind of look that was more like my older paintings: very layered, very painterly. I felt I had moved past that in my work, but I felt like I needed to be open to the parameters of the project, you know. I didn't want to be too closed-minded in my thinking. I thought that doing this project would help me expand the ways I approach things, but it ended up being a disaster. It just wasn't a good project for me. They kept telling me to add drips and dumb street-type shit like that. I kind of threw my hands up toward the end and just quit working on it. Thank god they dumped it before it ever came out…knock on wood…you never fucking know what people will pull. I'll see that busted-ass shit at Urban Outfitters next week.

RM: And you know what happens most of the time? These companies get rejected by their first-choice artist, and they go on trying to find someone who emulates the original. What they're after is simply the impression of working with an artist of some sort. It's rarely a particular artist. So, as you mentioned earlier, you're more inclined to work with a company that is down with what you specifically are trying to do with your work. Has there been an instance where a company has approached you with a project that you hadn't previously considered doing, but the opportunity presented something new that you were psyched about?

DALEK: There hasn't really been anything all that amazing thrown my way yet. Commercially speaking, I want someone to ask me to design an amusement park. How hot would that be? Space monkey mountain! But I'm just getting started.

RM: Are there any artists or companies that you've seen do a project that made you lose respect for that artist or company?

DALEK: Nothing that really jumps out at me. I like most of what I see.

"The most important thing for me when working with a company is to make sure they understand the culture they want to be supporting and that, in return, the work or the concept will not suffer by being commercialized."

EASE

EASE

José Parla (EASE) is an artist who lives and works in Brooklyn, New York.

RM: What corporate-sponsored projects have you been involved in and why?

EASE: I have been involved with a program called Truth. I basically thought it was great to send out a message that is informative to youth about what's really in tobacco. They're not saying to kids, "Don't smoke." They're telling kids what's really chemically in cigarettes and all the corruption involved behind the tobacco industry.

RM: What exactly was your involvement with this Truth project?

EASE: I taught kids how to use art materials, hung out answering questions they had about art and was really just a person the kids could draw inspiration from.

RM: Was this an after-school program? Were you paid? Was it volunteer? What was in it for Truth?

EASE: I have taught students after school before and worked with city youth programs in Atlanta, Bronx, and Brooklyn as a volunteer both during and after school. With Truth, it was different. There was pay involved, and it was based on events. One event was at Washington Square Park, which also included Lee Quinones, Jam Master Jay, Crazy Legs, and Rock Steady Crew. It was an afternoon party for the public, mostly for the kids. I was teaching the kids to paint with spray paint. Truth gets down with the street credibility of the artist to attract the kids and give them information about corruption from smoking and tobacco companies.

RM: What are the motives for artists and corporations to work together?

EASE: Some corporations and artists can meet halfway and agree on things that benefit both parties. Corporations want an artist's credibility.

The artist wants to make money but not sacrifice the true style or culture. The trade-off can be negative unless, as an artist, you take precautions and watch out for the bait-and-switch routine a lot of companies use. They tell you one thing and it's not that at all.

RM: I love the phrase "bait-and-switch." It really does happen all the time, and, to be fair, it is often the result of companies being made up of many different people who are not communicating well with each other. As an individual, you have to deal with a corporate beast that has many different heads attached to it, and so there can be a lot of mixed messages, making it difficult to come to an agreement.

EASE: On the other hand, if both parties agree, then it can be positive for the artist in a lot of ways. First, it can mean financial support to make a project more solid than if it's done out of the artist's own pocket. You can have the company's people take care of almost all the logistics for an event or exhibit, and the artist can concentrate on the art and not stress out doing all the organizing and all that. If everything works out well, depending on what the agreement was, it can also mean that there's good PR involved, and the artist can get appropriate press, which can amount to more opportunities. Of course, there is the job fee. If things work out, you'll get the money you asked for. It has its benefits only when things are done professionally. And it all depends on how realistic an artist or a corporation is being to the other.

RM: That's a pretty solid list of positives. Can you give an example of a relationship with a company that has worked out for you?

EASE: A company from Japan named Balance

Wear Design I work with is doing what they say they're going to do. We have lawyers to interpret and make contracts in English and Japanese, and there is a good vibe about our business. The most important thing for me when working with a company is to make sure they understand the culture they want to be supporting and that, in return, the work or the concept will not suffer by being commercialized.

RM: You also worked with Agnès B., and that seems to be a relationship that has been built on mutual respect. Can you explain the different projects you've done together?

EASE: Agnès B. presented our show titled *Boomerang* on April 12, 2002. It was with Lee Quinones, RoStarr and myself. *Boomerang* is a show about our views on the September 11th attacks on the World Trade Center. Organizing the whole event took a lot of effort, but we also had Chris Apple, press manager for Agnès B. help out with everything, and Agnès herself likes to help out as well. The show took place at her old Soho store in front of her men's shop, which, after being emptied out, looks like a perfect gallery space. It's huge and has two massive floors. We showed paintings upstairs and slides downstairs. Agnès came over to see the artwork before it was hung, and she took her time and looked at the space. This was the same afternoon of the show's opening. We had no idea that later on that evening there would be nearly two thousand people there. It was the most amazing crowd of people, mixing all the downtown socialites with the old and new school writers from all NYC, and many artists were there. Even homeless people were in there having the time of their life. Before the doors even opened, it looked like there was not going to be enough champagne, Agnès ordered some more with no hesitation. She wanted everyone to have a great time. She actually partied with all of us all night until the show was over.

RM: I want to touch upon this idea of commercializing the art. What does that mean to you, and is it necessarily a bad thing?

EASE: I'm making paintings that are personal in subject matter, so if a company wants to use the entity of my style of painting to sell products, then that is commercializing the style or technique. Does the subject matter remain silent? For example, a vodka company wanted to make billboards of my work for Las Vegas, Los Angeles, and Miami. The mock-up they showed me was wack. They changed the colors of my work, and I was not happy about it. They offered little money and demanded a lot of work. I wrote my proposal, which was not cheap, and that's when negotiations stopped. At the end of the day, they wanted to market their vodka to an age group of 21 to 25. As far as commercial art being good or bad, that depends on the artist and the specific project.

RM: It seems like that vodka company acted abusively, and it's admirable that you walked away. What other projects, if any, have you had to walk away from?

EASE: I also had to walk away from a show I was invited to be a part of in Japan. I was asked to paint on skateboards, but I really didn't think my work would fit.

David Ellis

David Ellis (SKWERM) works in various media, including painting, sculpture, installation, performance, film, and video. Ellis' work often addresses the intersection of urban and rural culture. The worlds of hip-hop, graffiti, and jazz interact with the landscape and culture of Ellis' rural upbringing.

RM: Have you ever worked with a company or corporation?

DE: When I was in school, in order to pay the bills and the rent, I would freelance by working on music videos, and that led to album covers. So I was working with record labels.

RM: Do you feel that that work was tied to your personal work?

DE: Sometimes it was like, "Here's this idea. Let's paint this room green," and obviously that's not related to my work. But over time, as people began to see what I was working on personally in the studio, I was asked to bring that into their mix. We're talking about '91, '92, '93.

RM: What are some of the things you took away from working on those early videos?

DE: That way of working has influenced my work. The method behind it—like the idea of building sets and making real theatrical things. Working on the sets had a direct relationship to doing graffiti and doing walls in a way for me that's like theater. I look at work that's done on the streets as theater—like transforming the space. I was learning tricks to rock really big pieces quickly, and I learned all the techniques of some of the old scenic painters.

RM: Tell me about the projects that are more directly linked with corporations or situations whereby you're co-branding yourself with corporations? Have you had to deal with those situations?

DE: For me, that would probably have started three or four years ago in Japan with a skateboard company that did a lot of clothing for that market. The company had a headhunter in New York who's actually a really good friend. So, he was interested in my work for a while, and I

would just crank out designs. When they don't ask you to do anything specifically, when there's no direction from the client whatsoever—it's just do whatever you want, bring whatever you want—it's going to be on a shirt, but it's a commission then that's all cool. There's a major difference between that and someone who's like, "Well, we've got this band, and they're this age, and they want this kind of thing. You know, we're going for red…" That shit sucks.

RM: Does that depend on whether or not you put your name to it?

DE: Yeah, I definitely have weird feelings about it. I don't know if I actually have navigated it. I think I'm learning from mistakes. I don't think I've always thought about that too far in advance, and I think sometimes it gets mixed up. I've always wanted to just make art. I've always had ideas that don't really fit any sort of salable model, and that's an important thing for me in that, like almost everything I've done in the last three or four years, even with Barnstormers, it's all really been not-for-profit. It's been about experiences. It's been about public work. It's been about putting our own money into these projects. It's been about looking for grants, and at the end of the day, it's been about something that gets buffed. It's not really like Barnstormers makes little salable things. I just had a show where pretty much 100% of the stuff I made the dealer (Jessica Murray Projects in Brooklyn) couldn't sell. I made a huge fucking mural that was top to bottom in this space, and I did this giant sound system with gourds all over the room, and it was all one thing. You couldn't really break it down and sell it. So, I probably won't be having a show there again.

RM: What have you learned from some of the mistakes you've made?

DE: Some of the mistakes include saying "yes" all the time. I think one of the biggest mistakes is being hungry, and I think one of the things I'm learning from watching some of the older cats like Futura and these guys is that they do very well by saying "no" all the time. I feel that things have gone really fast in the last couple of years. I don't have a lot of regrets in terms of the quality of work, but I do have maybe some regrets on the compensation. Maybe there could have been more bargaining and more leveraging…

RM: Any relationships that have gone sour?

DE: I'm not sure any of them have gone sour yet. I've always felt pretty well compensated. I don't really keep track of what's happening in Japan, and I'm not sure if they made money on the stuff that I did for them. Then again, I don't have any way of knowing. All I know is that I was paid decently for the time I put into that work, and I was taken care of very well when I was there. I think part of their business practice is to roll out the red carpet when you're in town, and you feel respected a lot more than you would here in New York. It's almost the opposite here. I guess maybe I feel that some of the choices I've made early on in Japan were with…I guess you could almost say they were mobsters who have control of certain branches of the media and can guarantee press and coverage of whatever events. It was always like there was an event that was sort of piggy-backed with a line of shirts that these guys were selling. It would be focused on a happening or an event where there would be bands playing, and the Barnstormers did live painting. It was great at that

time, because I got to travel to a place I hadn't seen. Now I've seen it almost too much. I've been to Japan more than I ever imagined I would. I've been twelve times, and I've forged some great relationships with some of my favorite artists in the world. So, I don't know if I'm actually that mad about it, but I think maybe I was over-saturated in some lesser, more sort-of frowned-upon publications. There's a certain class system in Japan that I'm starting to understand a little more. In those magazines, I'm often called a "street artist" or "graffiti artist." That happens here, too, and I always try to not depict myself in that way, because that's not where I am. I'm not out there hanging off rooftops doing stuff. I would love to for the thrill, but I'm thirty-two. I'm not sixteen.

RM: What do you look for in a relationship with a company?

DE: I don't know how many companies you can really believe in. Companies are out to make money. People get fucked somewhere along the chain. Somewhere in that company's process, people are getting screwed. Even my friends' companies—I think their production might definitely support some sweatshops and stuff that might not be so great. What do I know? Look at corporations like X&X.

RM: How did that X&X project come about?

DE: There's an art director who recommended our work to a small ad agency who pitched doing a Barnstormer-esqe thing. They had these photos of our work. They just saw this incredible situation being produced on a large scale—people covered in paint—and that excited the photographers. Even the people at X&X were like, that could be great for our image. Fashion always invents some sort of thing. It's always sort-of making up something that's fantasy—invents it or steals it. Often times, they steal it.

RM: When I picked up the Barnstormer X&X shopping bag at the show, you cringed.

DE: I guess I cringed because I saw their logo huge—their X&X logo huge on top of our work. I kind of cringe when I see the two-story billboard out here with "Jeans $10" on it.

RM: Who are the people in those ads?

DE: Originally there were supposed to be models, but a lot of the people in those ads are us. Here's another thing: contracts come with the big corporations, and we negotiated ours, but there was a time crunch, so we negotiated a contract, which, when it first was presented to us, wasn't going to include the United States. I thought that was a little more attractive—to not burn it so hard. I had no idea the scale of the campaign. I knew that it would somehow be easier for me to swallow if it wasn't happening here. There were a lot of things that I was sort of feeling bad about when I saw the contract. Things that I wanted to avoid. One was using the name "Barnstormers." No matter how you slice it up, it could not be "Barnstormers" for this campaign—even though you might have members of Barnstormers. This was obviously a fashion shoot. There were just weird moments when there was a model holding a can of paint with paint on her hands, moments when I felt really kind of manipulated. I would say things at that point like, "Bro, my impression was that we would paint. We would have our thing happening in the background, and they could shoot models." I realized they would have to shoot models, and there would be this distance

somehow. But it got kind-of woven together, and I don't think they're necessarily using "Barnstormers" on the ads. I did get that much as far as our name goes, but I know on their web site they talk about "Barnstormers" a little bit, which maybe is okay. I don't know how I feel about that.

RM: Do you feel they pulled one over on you?

DE: Yeah, I do. I feel that way. For example, three days after we're supposed to sign the contract and we're still debating different aspects of the contract, we find out it's talking about all these countries in Europe which we were cool with. But then in the 11th hour, X&X's lawyer says, "Oops! We left something out. It's going to run in the U.S., too." And when we said, "Well that changes everything!" they acted like we were supposed to know, even though it wasn't in the contract, that it was supposed to be like that all along. They actually gave us attitude. But in the end, we came to an agreement, and I think in general, it was good—definitely not in advertising terms, but in terms of the day rate for scenic painting or set design. That's kind of how we were looking at it in the beginning. Carah (von Funk) actually helped to wrap up that whole thing, and she got a lot of things cut down—like the time this thing can run is not long. It's only like three months, which seemed great to me. I thought, well, maybe people will just blink and miss it, and it will be gone.

RM: Do you want it to be missed?

DE: I just don't want this to be what we're about. It's not what we're about. We definitely did it for the money, and we did it for using that money to further projects that we do—not to sit back and

"There were just weird moments when there was a model holding a can of paint with paint on her hands, moments when I felt really kind of manipulated."

David Ellis (SKWERM)

retire, because we're not talking about a lot of money. As big as this campaign looks, the perception is going to be "Oh yeah. Barnstormers have sold out. They're paid." I'm sure people are saying that, and that's fine, because this helps us to be out there painting barns.

RM: You've also taken advantage of the exhibition space, because you're painting in that space and making another video. Is that video for them?

DE: No, not at all. We convinced them that our process involves time-lapse painting, and if we do a show, part of that show has to be time-lapse painting. In order to do it in their space, we need camera rentals etc. No one was paid a fee that I know of, but we wanted to get all the materials.

RM: Now that there's an association between X&X and Barnstormers, is it something you have to deal with?

DE: Yeah, we'll see. I guess on the good end of it, we've gotten some exposure on New York One. So, everybody who watches New York One might find out about what we do. That might help us get grants.

RM: Was that coverage outside of the X&X show or related to it?

DE: It was more on us, and they focused on how the Barnstormers are using that space to work with the Art Start Kids. That was their angle: We're a group that is giving back in some way.

RM: What is Art Start?

DE: They provide a space for kids after school, but it's more than that. They provide computers and resources and people who can teach kids Photoshop, Final Cut Pro, and other editing programs. It's not structured, but it gives kids a focused place to actually learn some skills and maybe learn some programs that might get them a job. They have a whole recording studio where kids can go record stuff. They can also learn engineering. What we're doing is kind of like a mentorship program. We try to open it up and actually take a couple of days to sit down with the kids and work. We did a thing where we silk screened a silhouette of a barn on a big piece of paper. Everybody sat down, and we did these paintings with the kids. We would pass the drawings after a little bit of time, and the kid would be working on someone else's drawing—figuring out how to deal with that space, and it was fun.

RM: You were involved with Art Start before X&X, so how did they get involved?

DE: Carah had been pushing the Art Start thing for some time, and I had been wanting to do a project with kids. So it fit. We brought the idea of doing a workshop in the X&X gallery, and after several meetings, X&X got involved. I guess they saw the obvious merits of the program as well as a PR angle, so they donated. They printed up 1,000 shirts that the kids had done that they're selling for ten bucks each, and 100% of the proceeds go to Art Start. So, they're giving back. They're trying to support it in that way.

RM: Do you think there could be a situation where a company that's for profit might have the same philanthropic agenda as Art Start?

DE: That would probably happen more on a foundation level. I have applied for a lot of grants from these kind of foundations, and I haven't gotten much response. But then again, I'm not the best grant writer.

RM: Would you accept a proposal from a corporation to fund Barnstormers with their logo on it?

DE: We've had that opportunity, and hell no. I think it's funny that when you went down with us you painted "YOUR AD HERE," because it was almost addressing that before it actually happened to us.

RM: Do you think there would be a way of taking that money and using it to your advantage?

DE: We were once sponsored by Gravis. This one really sucked. Oh, the thing I wanted to say about contracts, just a note for this interview, is that in the contract I can't say anything bad to discredit X&X publicly.* But there's a time frame on that, so we'll have to look at that, because we may have to put "a large clothing company" for every time we say X&X. But I guess, Gravis, well, I never signed any contract, so fuck 'em. They've actually got a really nice guy who's a marketing director who is young and gets what we do. He's just likeable. He's a really fucking nice guy. They flew seven Barnstormers to Miami for some big music festival that I didn't really know anything about. We're all painting these giant canvases as part of this event. We had done events like this before with Giant Step for fuckin' less than what the materials cost five, six years ago. It was fun, but with this event, the day we all got to the hotel we knew there was something up. We were told, "I want to tell you guys this sort-of came up. There's a photographer here. She's going to be taking pictures of Ro-Starr, whom, incidentally, we sponsor." I didn't really know what that meant, but Ro was under contract with these guys. So, the other six of us are kind of like with Ro doing this event, and they were like, "If the photos come out good, we don't know anything yet, but if they're good, we may use them for a little cam-

paign. It won't be much of a big deal." I just like stopped him in his tracks in front of everybody. The whole crew was there, and I said, "If it is used in a campaign, then there needs to be adequate compensation. There are ethical guidelines on this shit, and I'd be glad to help you work out what those are, but it has to be ethical. It has to be official," and he's like, "Oh yeah, I'm sure it will be." Then ads ran in fucking everything. I know what ad space costs, and it was really bad. I told him that this was not really what we wanted to do, and after long conversations with everybody doing research and finding out what we should get, I just said, "Give what you can to the barn painting project and make a corporate donation to the New York Foundation of the Arts so that in the future, when we go down south, maybe we'll have enough money for a hotel room." The donation was a far cry from what any reasonable promoter would pay for a publicized live painting event—never mind the fact that they stretched it out into a huge print campaign. Motherfuckers. That was sloppy. It just wasn't handled well, and it was disrespectful. That's part of our problem—being seduced by cats who come off as being part of the scene. I think all of us are growing and learning from these experiences and the more we can talk about it with each other and figure it out, the better.

RM: Are there any artist-corporation relationships that you've seen that made you change your mind about the company or the artist?

DE: Well, KRS One did…what was it? Sprite, I think, and he's one of the greatest fucking anti-everything, anti-establishment artists there was—at least when I was a kid. He and Public

Enemy were talking about the most grass-roots shit, and to see him... I forget what it was, so maybe that's a good thing. I remember KRS and not the company that he was pitching. But the fact is that he did it. But musicians impact the world community a hell of a lot more than Barnstormers. We're subculture. We'll always be subculture. I think we're very fortunate to have gotten opportunities to do stuff for Sesame Street, and the thing I just did with Nike was cool, because they really took a lot of the videos Barnstormers had done to another place that makes me want to do more shit like that.

RM: Do you think doing these projects prevents you from being taken seriously?

DE: I think about Keith Haring, and I think about Andy Warhol when those questions come up. I think in some ways, part of their success happened simultaneously with them also doing an Absolut Vodka bottle, doing a fucking Swatch, or whatever. I think that in different ways they got up. But honestly, right now, I just want to work. I have more fun just making work. It's like having too many paintings up in your studio. You feel like you've accomplished something. I'm always trying to find ways to get my walls blank again—to get rid of my shit. It's the same thing when you see your shit everywhere, and you start to feel like you've really accomplished a lot. Well, not really. Accomplishing a lot is doing it everyday. Accomplishing a lot is making the work, regardless of whether or not you reach a lot of people. I like to see the artists with whom I'm in constant contact come into the studio and see that I've done a new thing in the work—that I've invented something in the work. And I like going to their studios and seeing them do the same thing. Even if we're not physically painting on the same canvas, we're having a dialogue, and I want to get back to that. I want to get out and see more studios and the artists I really believe in. That process doesn't have shit to do with whether I have a billboard somewhere or I don't have a billboard somewhere. Or whether I have a show, or I don't have a show. That's the only reason I do it, and that's what I live for.

*

"...You and Artists agree that during the Term and for a period of six (6) months thereafter, none of the Artists will make any statements that disparage or reflect unfavorably on X&X, the Campaign or the Fashions. You and Artists further agree that Artists will not authorize or release advertising matter or publicity, or give interviews that make reference to the Artists or any of the Artist's engagement hereunder, without our prior written approval, except for favorable and positive references to X&X during interviews or in personal publicity...."

"I know that for me, living in the absolute country from age 10 to 19, MTV and magazines were the only cultural outlets I had."

Brendan Fowler (BARR)

Brendan Fowler

In 1997 Brendan Fowler published Sex Sells Magazines, *a book-zine that documented artists' lives in their own words. Since then, he has worked with various artists and galleries on numerous projects. He lives and works in Los Angeles and performs under the name BARR.*

RM: What corporate-sponsored projects have you been involved in and why?

BF: Ok, well, right now I'm simultaneously doing two projects funded by a company that I have always revered as the motherfucker of all motherfucker fuck-people-over-and-hide-behind-bullshit corporate companies: Nike. (Note: I've really been racking my brain, and I feel like this is my first real brush with corporate work stuff like this. I have worked a lot with art galleries [mainly Alleged and Deitch], and aside from some product support at openings, I can't recall any real corporate involvement in any gallery stuff I've done). So, these two projects are: Nike is giving, maybe I shouldn't say how much, but it's under $30,000 to support this Barry McGee/Thomas Campbell/Phil Frost (w/Alife) art show at Roberts and Tilton Gallery in Los Angeles. $1,500 of it is set aside as my budget with which to make a catalog for the show. I'm lucky in that it's up to me how I wish to spend it (ie: the cheaper the production, the more money I get paid to do it).

RM: You should turn around and sell ad space in the catalog to other shoe companies: $1,500 isn't going to get you very far in producing a catalog, so you should go back to Nike and say, "In order to do this thing right, I've sold the back cover to Adidas." Do you think this is a real possibility, or does the catalog have to be a "Nike" product?

BF: Well, it's not really a Nike product. I have no intention of putting any mention of Nike anywhere in the whole thing. It's going to be this 100+ page monster fucked-up crazy object catalog in an edition of 300 or 400, and Nike/the gallery doesn't know it maybe, but I'm actually going to get it Xeroxed for very cheap (read: free), so the

$1500 is basically my fee. But you're right. Were it being offset printed, $1500 wouldn't mean shit, and honestly I think that that's what Nike thinks the money is going to. I don't think they counted in my design/labor fee or really even thought about the catalog budget realistically, and in that case, the Adidas idea would be so hot and fully right on. But, that's cool—I feel like I'm getting around them.

RM: And the other project?

BF: Also, I'm going to assist the artists in the actual production/installation of some of the work. But the main thing is that I'm getting the $1,500 for the catalog. (Incidentally, if it's true that their shoes only cost about 80 cents a pair to make, $1,500 is like two thousand pairs of shoes for them.) And the other project is Nike is giving Steve Powers a bunch of money (I don't know how much—I haven't asked.) to make art in LA. Apparently they had no idea what his plans were, and he is employing me and another graff kid to assist him in doing full-on illegal graffiti all over LA. Then they're going to have a nice fully catered/stocked party at their very exclusive "Blue/Presto" House in Venice Beach for Steve where he shows pictures of the damage.

RM: This is a great solution to the corporate-sponsorship paradox. We both love Steve and his work, and I'm sure he doesn't give a shit about Nike's response. However, just to play devil's advocate and provoke a discussion, do you think his actions are at all irresponsible, and, in the end, if the goal is to share his work/vision/message with as many people as possible (and that may be a gross assumption), then why doesn't he just "get with the program" and play nicely with Nike?

After all, Nike has incredible distribution channels and could ultimately help Steve reach more and more people. Again, for argument's sake.

BF: Well, Nike does have those channels, but in the end (and the middle and the beginning, for that matter) they are really Nike's channels, which work by Nike's rules. Some artists I know always take a stance of "Fuck them, I am absolutely not going to have any involvement with [insert any mega-corporate entity here] at all, no way!" And, you know, I can fully appreciate where they are coming from. But I have to give it to Steve; when he is offered an opportunity to work with a big-ass corporate company he says "Now, can I do something that allows me to make whatever point I want to make, without compromising for the company?" If it seems like it's not going to happen, he moves on. But you know, sometimes, just like in this Nike thing, the situation happens to be perfect. He is getting the money, and all they really want to see is some end result so they can show it at their clubhouse. But what I am saying is that if Steve were to work "nicely" within every company's vision to reach more people, he would be working their vision, and he would almost every time have to leave like 90% of his vision at the door.

RM: This may be wishful thinking, and perhaps it happens more in the recording industry, but is it really not possible for an artist to work with a large corporation to share his work with the world? I'm afraid there really is no model for real artists to reach a mass audience, or is there?

BF: Well, I don't know what the model would be, but I feel like it could be done. I guess that as lame and watered-down and silly as Shepard Fairey's "Andre The Giant" thing has become, he is actually doing a really amazing job of getting it out to the world. I think that a lot more kids know about him than most punk bands on indie labels. So he could sort-of be considered a model. Granted, he has turned it into his own highly commercial sort of venture, but he's done it pretty much on his own terms, and in the end he has really worked hard and it's happening for him. I think that it can be done. So, the thing is that as much as I think Nike is fucked for many reasons, the money that they are giving to these two projects is money that wouldn't be there otherwise, and in both cases it has been the difference between the project happening and the project not happening.

RM: On that note, do you really think there is no alternate source of funding for such artists? Grants? Foundations? Patrons? Investors? I'm curious if these corporations really are the last hope in funding art projects.

BF: Well, you know, I think that it's kind of three things. 1) Grants and foundations are maybe drying up a bit right now, so it's more work to get them; 2) Private citizen patrons are wanting to spend less money on arts because the economy is fucked right now, and 3) Since corporations operate sort-of like private foundations in that there may be a smaller and quicker decision-making body deciding where they spend their money, they may be easier to deal with than some grant boards. Also, corporations usually pay other people to do things like trend forecasting, where it's a job to say "We should work with so-and-so, because he/she is hot right now and would benefit our company's image." It's sort-of like a corporation might really readily take the idea of street cred into consideration, whereas a grant board is probably going to be like "whatever" about it.

RM: That's a good point about selection process. Corporations tend to follow trends and be told whom to select (by either magazines or forecasters) whereas foundations that give grants tend to do so based on merit. Or maybe this is naïve, and foundations are just as political as corporations and they'll receive recommendations from board members, etc. Is there really no way to win if you'd like have your work funded based on the work itself?

BF: Well, you know, I think that if you are really truly kicking ass and working hard at putting yourself out there (whatever that may entail), you are going to get rewarded. I mean, nobody is going to help you out if they don't know about you. The flip side to that is that a lot of shitty artists get shine because they're good hustlers, but in the end, if you're good and you're not fully inept at dealing with people, I think you can get something going. Also, to back up a bit, neither case has been a direct Nike ad (only in the first case on the show poster it says "with generous support from [swoosh icon]"). I can honestly say that I would not willingly appear in a Nike ad or design an ad campaign for them.

RM: Ok, Brendan, I'm Mr. Nike, and I'd like to pay you $100,000 to create this campaign. I don't want your image or your name attached to it. Wouldn't that be a nice chunk of change with which to publish your next project? Or can dirty money never be washed clean?

BF: Well, it comes down to if you want to get paid to help Nike. Doing an ad campaign is creat-

ing something to help their company. It's like working in a gun store when you don't believe in firearms. I think that in their case, as I understand the company, I would not do it. (However, let me also note that I never thought I would wear Nike's again, either, but Steve Powers just gave me a free pair of Air Force Ones, a model that I didn't even particularly like, and I'm fully wearing them. I actually really like the pair of shoes a lot. I might cut the swooshes off, but I'm fully stoked on the shoes he gave me.)

RM: So, you're making a distinction between Nike ads and Nike sponsorship. Ads send a more overt message, and a credit line on a poster is more subtle. However, conceptually, aren't they one and the same? Or is there a real difference?

BF: Yes, a big difference. I know people who have been in a company's ads but would never use that company's product, because they think the product sucks. But that few grand they got paid for being in the ad sure didn't suck. (I've done it myself, but they were kind-of inoffensive smaller companies, if there is such a thing.) Putting your face or your trademark image in an ad says, "I endorse this product, or at least got paid to pretend that I do." Using their money and giving them a small credit says "so-and-so used X CORP's money and gave them a small credit." In both cases the artist and the company are represented on the page, but it would be like if you switched the roles of plaintiff and defendant in a courtroom. Both sides would still be in the room, but there would be a really big difference in the proceedings.

RM: That's a great analogy. Two sides, same courtroom, and all anyone wants is to be served up some justice. So, who's the judge?

BF: The public. Or your peers, which is probably the only segment of the population that really cares. It would be so rad if people cared a lot about these things. If they did, it would be harder for companies to be fucked in the first place. But in the cases of the art show and the catalog and the ESPO thing, I have decided that if it's the only way it's going to get done, I am going to use their fucked-up blood money to make my projects happen.

RM: So, you're taking on a kind-of Robin Hood role? Is this in the service of bringing the work to an audience that otherwise wouldn't be able to afford it?

BF: Absolutely. Or at least making a project happen that couldn't happen at all (without the funding for space/materials/shipping/labor, etc).

RM: What are the motives for both artists and corporations to work together?

BF: Well, in my understanding, artists are usually doing it to get financial/material support for their projects. The corporation's money is going to enable some art that maybe could not have happened without the financial/material support of the corporation. And the corporations are doing it to seem compassionate, creative, or supportive of arts/culture; or perhaps they really want to support creative culture; or they just want tax write-offs.

RM: There is a range of motives for these companies, and every case is different.

BF: I think that in the case of Nike, they wish to link up with artists who will give them some more street cred and can maybe even inform their products. Also, I know that in Nike's case, $22,000 is really a pretty small drop in the bucket for them, and their subtle mention on the poster alone, which will go out to however many art people, is really very good advertising for their money.

RM: Yes, twenty-two grand is perhaps even insulting. Obviously, the parties involved agreed to accept this amount, and admittedly, we don't know all the details. However, can you imagine an amount that would have been unacceptable?

BF: Well, I think it was like, "Let's get as much as possible with the least expected in return." If they would have said, "We'll give you 100 grand, but you have to have a Nike swoosh on every wall," the response definitely would have been, "We'll pass." One of Nike's main competitors offered $4,000 to sponsor the show, and if Nike hadn't beaten that, the gallery would have gone with the other company's $4,000. But if Nike offered $4,500 and Swatch came out of left field with the highest offering of $7,000, there would definitely be a Swatch logo on the poster. I probably would also not be making the catalog like I am right now, cause that's not the number one priority in terms of what to do with the money.

RM: So in this specific instance, the sponsor's participation is really based solely on financial contribution. Let's say a company doesn't have a lot of money to offer (or buy its way in) but is a company that the artist is down with. Can you point to any examples of mutually beneficial and equal contribution artist-corporation relationships?

BF: Phil Frost paints with White-Out pens, which starts to get expensive pretty quick. The White-Out company sent him a case of White-Out.

RM: You produced an incredible book some years ago called *Sex Sells Magazines*. If I remember correctly, there were a few small ads in the book, and the production and distribution were limited. Would you have accepted a corporate sponsor or underwriter for the book in order to have gotten it out to more people?

BF: Absolutely. Yes. I had just graduated high-school, and I really didn't know what I know now about acquiring that kind of financial backing. I had already done a smaller version, *Sex Sells Magazines Number One*, and I was still operating under the indie zine model: At the most, you get ads from indie record labels and such to offset your printing costs. If I had any idea about how to get one source to pay for the thing and get more copies made and shipped out, I would have been there. I have always wanted to spread information to the kids. The more the better.

RM: The more kids the better? In the end, does it really come down to the number of people you reach as opposed to the quality of people you reach? I hate to put "the people" in qualitative terms, but I do want to ask you this: Would you rather reach 10 million semi-retarded MTV viewers who may not appreciate your message, or 1,000 like-minded individuals at a gallery opening who "get" what you're doing?

BF: Well, ideally, I've always wanted to give the "semi-retarded" MTV viewers an option. I know that for me, living in the absolute country from age 10 to 19, MTV and magazines were the only cultural outlets I had. I taped 120 Minutes (the weekly MTV show of "alternative" music videos) every week, and if it weren't for that show, I would have been seriously fucking bumming.

For a lot of kids, MTV is all they have, and it's how they get turned on to a lot of stuff. Well, actually, now they have the internet, which I didn't have. The internet rules. Isolated kids all over find communities that they never could have found before. It's positive. But in answer to your question, in the end, Ryan, nobody has to like shit, so the rad thing to me would be to give the most people possible the chance to check shit out and decide for themselves, and that goes for semi-retards and hipster snobs alike.

"The idea of a major corporation looking at someone like myself is new. For example, I have a lot of Apple computers, but they've never given me any of them. And, by the way, they would be my ultimate dream corporate sponsor."

FUTURA

FUTURA

FUTURA is an artist who lives and works in Brooklyn, New York.

RM: I've been following your work for quite some time, and I'm impressed with your range of output: from album covers, to clothing, to canvases, to web sites, to animations, to figures, etc. How do you decide what projects to take on?

FUTURA: Throughout the last twenty years, I have tried to adapt and transition. The work I have created is representative of that journey and the situations in which I have found myself. That journey is ongoing and may always require changes in direction and/or my mode of travel. Thus, there needs to be a versatility in movement.

RM: Are there any corporate-sponsored projects that you've been involved in?

FUTURA: I don't have corporate sponsorship, in the classic sense. I'm not an athlete or a movie star. The idea of a major corporation looking at someone like myself is new. For example, I have a lot of Apple computers, but they've never given me any of them. And, by the way, they would be my ultimate dream corporate sponsor. I have, however, worked with a few high-profile companies in the last few years. The first is Levi's Japan, which is not worldwide. The other is Nike, which certainly is worldwide, but my project with them was limited to US distribution only. Most recently, I've done a new campaign with Calvin Klein, which also included DELTA and ESPO. In the case of both Nike and Levi's, the production was in numbers of under 1,000 units and very limited in distribution. But in the case of CK, the quantities are in the tens of thousands. I think this will be, by far, the biggest mainstream exposure I have had to date.

RM: With Levi's Japan, did you produce FUTURA jeans?

FUTURA: Not exactly, although the jeans did have a "FUTURA" label embedded beneath the actual "501 Original," and it was an intentionally torn label. That was a chance to provide characters, design and art direction to a jacket, jean and sweatshirt set. The three box set had a denim cover. Approximately 900 were produced and included a very original package design. After this series, which was my first work with the company, another follow-up project was offered, which I rejected. That was in 2000/2001. Last year, one of my extensions, "Futura Laboratories" used original Levi's jeans as a foundation for new character applications. This was a kind of double label for Japan only.

RM: What was the collaboration with Nike?

FUTURA: This year Nike started a campaign titled, "3's," using a variety of talent from various media. Artists are asked to choose a sneaker model and then elaborate to their creative end. In the first set of 3's, I have been included along with Eminem and Sarah Jessica Parker. My choice of model was the Blazer, which originates back in the '70s (much like myself). Also, my selection of the colorway/fabricway is representative of my personal aesthetic. The green, black, and olive colors are, in fact, a reference to the camouflage palette I have an affection for. The 1,000 numbered series (I got the first 50), was limited to US distribution only. The Nike collaboration was for a charitable event that raised money for the NYC Coalition for the Homeless. As for my newest Nike effort, check for the Dunk SB colorway/fabricway on Ebay.

RM: Are there corporate projects that you seek out and perhaps propose?

FUTURA: I would invite such projects if, in fact, any were offered. The fact remains that since I do not seek such support, it doesn't wind up knocking on my door. Obviously I'm ok with that for now. I mean, taking it all as things happen to fall into place is a mode of operation I often follow.

RM: I'm sure lots of companies are knocking! How do you decide when to answer the door?

FUTURA: OK, so some are knocking. You simply have to trust your judgment to make wise choices. It's also very easy to say, "No!" when you can pay your rent.

RM: What are the motives for artists and corporations to work together?

FUTURA: To spend large portions of their money to support the creative process, to take advantage of that possibility and spend that money in pursuit of one's dreams.

RM: For a lot of the other artists I'm interviewing, that does seem to be the model: take the corporate money and apply it to the "real" work, which is pursuing one's dreams. So, what corporate work do you do, and what are the dreams you are pursuing?

FUTURA: Looks as if I don't heed my own advice. I just don't have any huge plans with ideas to create the big project or to spend or make the big money. I'm just not that ambitious. But, I would also say that having a sneaker out with that big four-letter word isn't a nightmare. Maybe a dream would be to design the placement of all the corporate logos that would appear in a NASCAR racing vehicle.

RM: Has there ever been a case where you've changed your opinion of an artist because he or she has worked with a certain company?

FUTURA: Sure, that happens—but to varying degrees. You have to look at the specifics of who, what, where, and when. Often times, it's a question of respect or integrity. Some associations are certainly damaging and can fuel the fires for the haters who gravitate. But others, and the perceptions they convey, can have a positive effect.

RM: I've been hearing a lot of stories about companies taking advantage of artists and abusing the relationship. Has this ever happened to you?

FUTURA: Fortunately, no. That hasn't happened to me, or at least not in that venue. But I've heard stories too. My days of being used, victimized, and exploited are long since over. The "graffiti" art movement (for lack of a better word) of the '80s was a fertile ground for such activity. In that context, and let me be frank, I don't think the rape and sodomy of any individual is romantic.

GREEN LADY

Green Lady was founded in 1995 by Todd St. John and Gary Benzel, who are based in Brooklyn and San Diego, respectively. Green Lady is an independent clothing label and producer of exhibitions. (greenlady.com)

RM: What corporate-sponsored projects have you been involved in and why?

TSJ: We're probably a little different than some of the other people you are talking to in that the majority of the work we create is something close to what I'd call "commercial art"—either products created for one of our clothing lines (Hunter Gatherer or Green Lady) or as a collaboration with a company—a client-type relationship. We have done more gallery shows in the last few years, but we've sort-of fallen into that rather than sought it out. A couple of those shows have had some sort of sponsorship element attached to them.

RM: Can you tell me what some of those sponsorship elements have been?

TSJ: We've had some stuff commissioned or bought by a company for a space they own. It seems like most group things we've been in have had some kind of underwriting or sponsorship behind them. There's been a decent amount of product design we've done with other companies, where the end product had both their name and our name attached.

RM: Your art production is unique in that you operate as partners under the name "Green Lady." Or do I not have this correct? Can you spell out for me what you do, with whom, for whom, under what name(s), and why?

TSJ: OK. Gary Benzel and I started Green Lady primarily as a clothing line around 1994. HunterGatherer was launched in 2000. Working under an alias was always interesting to us, because it doesn't insert our own identities directly into the picture. It essentially creates a brand, and people have a different relationship with a brand than with an individual. Commercial art and design is a largely anonymous medium, and we liked the idea of playing with that anonymity—creating slightly more thoughtful work in an environment where people might not be expecting it. We never really sought out gallery shows, but once we started getting invited to do to them, we decided to collaborate in a similar way as we had working on the clothing. Though, there is a shift in how we deal with the medium and the context. We consider ourselves to be a kind of artist, and not simply as a design firm, especially in the case of Green Lady. We have never created client work under that name. When we started out, we purposely avoided the fine-art world, because we felt it was not as accessible to us or the backgrounds we came from. What people would call street art, skateboard art, etc. all sort-of avoided the category of fine art, and we opted to make work that was more affordable, accessible, and readily available. That is primarily where we were coming from.

GB: The way we approach our work has to do with it being enjoyable. We started working on projects together in college. We also have a similar sensibility with aesthetics and subject matter, which is one of the reasons we started collaborating back when. In most cases, the images we put out do start with one of us thinking of something as an individual, but the other will edit, add to, or make improvements.

RM: I like the idea of art groups where the members surrender their individual identities to the group's brand. Obviously, there's a precedent for this in art history, especially more recently with Art Club 2000, General Idea, and let's throw

"The ultimate motivation is understanding that a lot of people's art experience isn't coming through galleries and museums."

GREEN LADY

Fischerspooner in there as well as graffiti crews. Do you align yourselves with any of these groups and see Green Lady as part of this history, or do you see Green Lady as defining some kind of new category of art group?

TSJ: I don't think our intention was ever to necessarily promote the brand as an art group, more just as a somewhat anonymous brand at the beginning. It changed slightly when we did the first installation pieces, but our original intention was more to work together on creating groups of designs for the entity or brand.

GB: We are making a new graffiti crew that only does graffiti on pictures in Photoshop.

RM: And on this note of anonymity, you mentioned earlier that you want to play with this idea. I'm curious about artists creating brands that parallel corporate brands that avoid individual accountability. In what ways does producing work under a brand name allow you more freedom? Or less freedom? Are you able to do things you wouldn't normally do under your individual names?

TSJ: Originally yes, but most people know it's us now, so the fun is over.

GB: I think the goal with that is to create good work without an individual's specific style or identity attached too much to the project, and that is where the group editing and decision making works for this project—by keeping the focus on what works best and is most interesting conceptually for the brand.

RM: And have your design backgrounds influenced your willingness to work with companies on various projects?

TSJ: On design jobs, a lot of what we do is collaborate with other people or companies, so no, it's not a foreign thing to us.

RM: What projects, specifically, has Green Lady been involved in where you've worked with a corporation?

TSJ: There was a show underwritten by a skate shoe company, and there's talk of an upcoming show in conjunction with a clothing company. There have been a few group things that had some sponsorship element. Not a lot though. There have been some co-branded products where outside companies had us do shirts or bags, etc., where both our name and their name were on the product.

GB: With the skate shoe thing, It was a very different thing than if Pepsi or IBM had been putting their stamp on the show. There have also been times where work we thought of as basically client-based was presented as a sort-of artist endorsement rather than a commissioned illustration.

RM: With the co-branded projects, I assume these were with companies you respected. What do you look for in a company you decide to work with?

TSJ: That it's a good match conceptually. As a small operation, there are certain things that are out of our reach to actually make without a lot of help from a bigger company. We look for a good amount of shared ideas and some mutual respect built up.

GB: In a perfect world, they are not making things that are bad for people and hopefully not exploiting people along the way.

RM: What are the motives for artists and corporations to work together?

GB: The motives for the corporations are to attach their name and image to the ideas and ideals expressed by an artist, or for the corporation to appear as part of an influential elite. For the artist, it may be a means of support to continue doing art. That book *No Logo* has a lot to say about why corporations want to sponsor and work with artists.

TSJ: For me, the decision to choose more commercial art instead of "fine art" had a lot to with the mass-produced and democratic aspect of it. Products and clothing produced in multiples, or video work that gets broadcast to millions of people, are very accessible and immediate art forms. Working with larger corporations has pluses and minuses, but it does allow you much more reach. The ability to connect with younger people, and people whose access to fine art may be limited, is really a strong motivator. I think of it as a "trickle-up" sort of cultural influence.

RM: So, the ultimate goal is to broaden your reach? Is this ever at the expense of the message?

TSJ: The ultimate motivation is understanding that a lot of people's art experience isn't coming through galleries and museums. The art that probably affected me the most was stuff that I experienced in high school or earlier. The ideas I absorbed at that age shaped a lot of my adult thinking. My parents really didn't expose me to fine art, and growing up in Hawaii, there wasn't much access to museums or galleries at all. So the "art" I took in was mostly images seen in magazines, comics, surf graphics, videos, posters for labels or bands, and the music itself—not always high-brow things, but a lot of times there were really sophisticated ideas that got slipped

in there. That definitely affected my decision to go into an art form that was as accessible as possible, and that could be available to people who grow up in similar situations. Which is a lot of people.

GB: We are from the streets!

TSJ: OK, if you don't mind, here's a question I have for you: Corporations have been one of the main underwriters of the arts for a very long time, and almost any major corporation has a program for contributing to the arts. What do you see as having changed in the recent past?

RM: I'm most interested when artists co-brand themselves with companies by producing such products as t-shirts, sneakers, figures, etc. It is this kind of sponsorship that is new, because companies are imposing their own identity onto the work. Instead of quietly underwriting projects as patrons, companies are creating their "artist limited-edition line" of this thing or that. Do such projects dilute the integrity of the work and/or the artist's "brand"? Who is using whom and what are the motives?

TSJ: I think this is kind of cyclical, but definitely more extreme now. Companies did this a lot in the sixties and in the eighties—think Swatch, BMW, Absolut, etc., with different categories of art. "Street Art", "Skate Art", etc. are popular now, but 10 years down the line, something else probably will be, and companies will be putting their money behind that. Keith Haring, Andy Warhol, and others at points had heavy collaborations with corporations, but it is has come back around again, probably more aggressively this time. Thomas Frank writes a lot about this sort of cross-pollination between corporate interests, and the creation and exploitation of counter cultures.

RM: Yes, I think corporations are treating these sponsorship arrangements more aggressively than ever before. There seem to be more "collaborations" between artists and companies that go beyond the simple, "Ok, decorate one of our watches, cars, or alcohol bottles." Now, you've got new and unique objects being made that are being equally authored by the company and the artists. Consequently, you've got a co-branding situation going on. Does this reflect the emergence of a new "product art" category, or a form of "diluted art" for the masses, or simply "new and improved" products?

TSJ: I think this has happened more with people from a "lifestyle" or "youth culture" background (skate, surf, street, graffiti, whatever) and less from the grad-school crowd. I don't think Paul McCarthy will be releasing collectible action figures any time soon, even though he should. I guess you end up with something that exists halfway between a subset of art and product design. I like your "product art" phrase. I think most of it isn't very deep conceptually but has appeal in its cultural references and a sort of object-fetishism. It's hard to say in general terms if those deals are good or bad. It depends on the artist having the sense to know whether they're being exploited or enabled.

RM: Yes, there is a difference between this trend being an organic, culture-based one as opposed to an academic one. Why do you think this difference exists?

TSJ: Maybe it operates in more of a pop realm, although that is starting to change. A lot of the stuff is (or was) more available to people via larger

production (like t-shirts/skateboards) or based on pricing for ordinary-income type folk.

GB: It seems to evolve more naturally and be less stodgily codified.

RM: This is exactly the gap I personally try to bridge with my own work, and a lot of times I do see education as the barrier. Is educating part of Green Lady's responsibility as you try to introduce to the world more thoughtful products?

TSJ: Very few of the things we produce contain anything that would actually qualify as intelligent. Friends of mine who are deeply entrenched in the fine-art world seem much more guarded about releasing "products" because of the considerations about how it affects the future collectibility of the rest of their work. That's a whole end of it that we're really not thinking about now, or ever really wanted to think about.

GB: Maybe it's taking an art approach to every-day stuff.

RM: I like your note about the creation and exploitation of counter cultures. With graffiti culture specifically, it seems that a lot of companies that target youth culture incorporate empty graffiti stylings into their products and messages. This, in turn, inspires kids to go out and tag not as a genuine form of expression, but rather with the hopes of perhaps being exploited and paid by some of those companies. Can you think of other examples of this cycle with other subcultures? Damn, that's a lame question, because it happens with virtually all subcultures. But perhaps you can expound upon this idea.

TSJ: Hold on, let me put down my Krylon… I don't really know specifically about that. I wasn't doing graffiti growing up. I do think that advertis-

ing and graffiti have always been heavily interrelated. Graffiti has a lot to do with rejecting the idea that because corporations have the most money, they are the only ones entitled to make their mark, or control public spaces. People are bombarded by images, mostly ones put out by companies. To create your own imagery in that environment through graffiti (or in our case, creating our own products) has a lot to do with a sense of empowerment, or reclaiming something that belonged to us all in the first place. When companies co-opt that, it may not be automatically bad, but if it's nothing more than a mannerist bite, then that's basically exploitive. Advertising and "culture"/"subculture" have become so intertwined at this point that I think it's sometimes hard to say where one starts and the other stops.
GB: The only real subculture that exists today are the secretive hippies who live quietly amongst us and weave macrame to barter.

Evan Hecox

Evan Hecox is an artist and graphic designer probably best known for his work for Chocolate Skateboards. He has also done work for clients such as Adidas, VW, Nike, Burton Snowboards, Pioneer and Carhartt. He creates drawings, paintings and prints, which have been exhibited internationally.

RM: What corporate-sponsored projects (exhibitions, objects, or commissions) have you been involved in and why?

EH: In the last year, I was involved with a travelling group exhibition sponsored by Etnies. I decided to do it because my work would be travelling to a lot of major cities, and there was money set aside for me to travel to some of the shows, so it sounded appealing.

RM: Was there any hesitation in being involved in a corporate-sponsored art show that was outweighed by the positive facts you mentioned? And if so, what were some of those concerns?

EH: With the Etnies show, part of the agreement was that each artist would paint on a shoe. I had some mixed feelings about this, since I don't normally paint on shoes, and I felt like this type of thing crosses the line to where the company's product has now become part of the artist's work. I approached the problem by covering my shoes in brown paper and tried to make them more of my own art-object. I also weighed my decision to be involved with the show based on other artists who were involved that I felt have integrity, like Mike Mills and Ed Templeton.

RM: Considering the context of your work is definitely important. I've heard companies speak of artists in terms of getting a "lead domino" so that others will fall in after. What other companies and projects have you worked with or on?

EH: I've designed a lot of skateboards, and I've done work for companies like Nike, Carhartt, Burton, and VW.

RM: With these commissioned pieces, have any of them been "Evan Hecox & [company]" projects, or are they work-for-hire?

EH: They were all work-for-hire type projects, none of them were branded with my name or anything. They just wanted my style of work and they weren't looking for any name identity.

RM: How do you make a distinction between the commercial work you do and your personal work?

EH: I try to make the two sides fit together as much as I can without being in conflict. The style of both my commercial and personal work is fairly similar, but sometimes the subject matter in the commercial projects is nothing like what I would choose for my own stuff. I've been paid to do portraits of pro basketball players, but I wouldn't do that on my own time. I like doing both, but my own work is what I care most about and what I really enjoy.

RM: To what extent do you take on commercial projects in order to just pay the bills? Can you describe the thought process behind trying to make the two sides fit together?

EH: Making money is definitely the primary consideration behind the commercial work that I do, but of course everybody has to work. I usually really enjoy my work, though, and I like the problem-solving aspects of design, taking a challenge, having certain limits, and coming up with a creative solution Fine art is satisfying on a more personal level and it's more expressive, but I also really like working with type and other design elements. Sometimes commercial projects force me into trying new and different things that I wouldn't have done on my own. I also really like having my work out there on posters and skateboards and t-shirts. It's great to see somebody walking down the street with a skateboard under their arm that I did or to see an album in a record

"With the Etnies show, part of the agreement was that each artist would paint on a shoe. I had some mixed feelings about this, since I don't normally paint on shoes..."

EVAN HECOX

store that I designed.

RM: How do you address the use of the "Evan Hecox" name in association with the work you do with/for corporations?

EH: I actually started out doing graphic design work and didn't start showing artwork in galleries until later on, so I've never felt that uncomfortable having my name and my work associated with companies. My actual name is not really on any of the work I do, but people usually recognize the work anyway.

RM: Instead of a signature per se, you've developed a signature style?

EH: That's correct.

RM: You make a distinction between doing graphic design work and showing artwork whereas the aesthetic of the two is essentially the same (or am I off here?). Besides the subject matter being a difference between the two, what are other, more conceptual differences? Is your work inherently about selling, or do you simply allow this agenda to be attached to the work?

EH: My own work has to do with my observations of the world and the way I feel about things. It has a lot to do with my way of seeing, and I focus on things that are some combination of ugly or beautiful or interesting to me. It has less to do with specific subject matter and more to do with my belief that all things in the world, even inanimate objects, are alive and connected to one another in some way and that all things that can be observed or felt deserve consideration. These types of ideas sometimes find their way into my commercial work, but more often I just adopt the stylistic traits of my personal work and apply them to things that don't really interest

me but that I have to do for a project.

RM: Why do you think your work has been appreciated in more of a fine-art context recently? Is this a world you've made concerted efforts to be in?

EH: Well, I've been invited to be in a lot of shows recently, so it has given people an opportunity to see more of my work in that context than before. I usually try to make my commercial work, especially my skateboards, have as much of a personal, artistic feeling as I can given the limitations. I think people have responded to this and it's sparked an interest in my paintings and prints. I've made a bit more of an effort recently to promote my own work, because if I can sell more of my artwork, then I can justify spending a larger amount of time doing it, and that would be nice. I also just like to share my work by showing it and not just have it hidden away in my studio.

RM: How do you decide what companies to work with?

EH: I try to make smart decisions on which companies I'll do work for and which ones I won't. I won't do anything that I think looks cheap or corny or support a product that I think is bad.

RM: What are examples of some products you would not want to be associated with?

EH: I once had an offer from an ad agency to do work for Old Spice and another for a brand of motor oil. These are not the type of things I want to do. My ideal projects are things like book covers, album covers, posters, or anything where I'm given a fair amount of creative freedom. I'd like to do some textile designs. I enjoy working with people whom I feel have similar views and creative ideas, like my friends at Girl Skateboards.

RM: What are the motives for artists and corporations to work together?

EH: By hiring artists and designers, companies can make themselves appear cooler than they actually are and successfully market their products. For the artist, there is usually a good deal of money to be made from doing this type of work. I do commercial work so that I can make a decent living for myself and my family, which I don't think I could do by just selling my paintings and prints.

RM: Do you ever do commercial work simply for the love of being involved in a consumer society and for trying to make a positive contribution in that world?

EH: Like changing the system from within? No. I don't think it's possible. I think that consumer society in America, which I'm afraid I'm a part of, is really vile. I think people in this country consume products as a form of self-expression and as a way of defining themselves which seems really unfortunate, and I don't want to contribute to it. I do think that good design has the ability to make the world a better place in some small way.

Matt Houston

Matt Houston opened a gallery/boutique called Houston *in Seattle in 1999 and* Return of Houston *in Tokyo in 2001. Matt currently works at a corporation and continues to operate Houston in Portland, Oregon. (wehaveaproblem.com)*

RM: What corporate-sponsored projects have you been involved in and why?

MH: I've worked on the Tokion Neo-Graffiti projects, which were sponsored by Houston, Agnès B.., and Adidas. Houston also worked on the Levi's X Futura collaboration and a t-shirt project for Levi's USA that never made it to market. Houston, while not a "corporation," has sponsored and collaborated with artists. For example, we produced a lamp with Geoff McFetridge, some prints on canvas by Ben Drury, a toy with Shawn Wolfe, a silkscreened edition for Ro-Starr, and a lot of t-shirts. Houston itself has been a corporate-sponsored project. From 1997 to 2002, it was sponsored by Microsoft, where I was employed. Their support was in the form of stock options and the use of their equipment. Houston got additional sponsorship from a Japanese clothing distribution company in 2001. We opened and operated a space called Return of Houston in Tokyo for a year. I've learned a lot from these corporate experiences, and working within them helps me with my art—which explores topics like fine art vs. commercial art, corporate branding, PR, marketing, advertising, production, etc. Every day at work, I'm broadening and shaping my vocabulary, and that's been much more valuable to me than using company equipment or exercising stock options.

RM: So why do you think other artists collaborate with corporations?

MH: I think they do it for any number of reasons: exposure; money; a favor; the opportunity to work in a medium that they can't afford or don't know how to manufacture, to work with someone specific at another company, or to work with a company they respect. I really don't think that this collaboration stuff is an issue. I've seen it written about a lot lately, to the point that even talking about corporate sponsorship is getting old. Nobody's twisting arms here. No corporation is forcing these artists into indentured servitude, right? If they don't want to do it, then they don't have to. It's as simple as that. It doesn't seem out of the ordinary that things would evolve like this. This genre of art we're talking about here was born out of skating, graffiti, and the ubiquity of design and design tools like personal computers. It's from board culture and graffiti culture, which are both rebellious by definition. There are tons of companies willing to turn, as Joe Strummer said, "rebellion into money," and the graf artists are an easy target. A lot of artists embraced the computer as a tool in the '90s. We shouldn't minimize the impact that this has had on this movement. Suddenly, the tools reserved for classically trained craftsmen and technology previously owned only by those with deep pockets were in the hands of the masses. I think that this accessibility empowered people to do design and create art, products, movies, and music, much more than they had before. Product designs, CAD drawings, etc. made "design" more of an artform. These artists now have the tools to do "professional" work and to email their toy designs to Japan. We are now able to communicate internationally both quickly and inexpensively and to do business over the Internet. This is important to a business whose target consumer is niche and small but also scattered around the world. The Internet helps incubate an international underground culture. This art is not following the rules, so it makes

"This genre of art we're talking about here was born out of skating, graffiti, and the ubiquity of design and design tools like personal computers… There are tons of companies willing to turn, as Joe Strummer said, 'rebellion into money.'"

MATT HOUSTON

sense that the artists and patrons wouldn't try to follow any pre-existing gallery structure. There are a lot of art forms that have their own systems—their own heroes and rites and vernacular. Galleries, for the most part, are exclusive and limited and reach a very small, elite audience. Working with a corporation spreads ideas faster and further. These artists view fame not through "critical acclaim" but rather through getting their tag around the world, and what better language to use than one of the most universal languages in the world—consumerism? And what better shopping mecca than Tokyo? It's a little bit like, who can piss on the most fire hydrants? It's still graffiti. It's still all about the style in which you do it. This generation was educated about the power of branding when they first looked down and realized they had someone else's name written on their asses: Calvin Klein. I first learned about merchandising because of Star Wars. I remember going to a K-mart to buy Darth Vader, but he was sold out. Those things stick with you. And those things get explored in places like art by a generation of artist who grew up with it. These niche cultures will get commodified at a faster and faster rate. Corporations will continue to target influencers and early adopters, will jump on trends, and will then work with those artists until the concept becomes passé. I can't tell you how many times I've seen this food pyramid chart drawn in meetings, where influencers are on the top and mainstream on the bottom. Information flow and "viral marketing." Small audience to big audience. They start at the top or near it as a target so the trend trickles down through the cultures via word of mouth. Right now, I think this art collabora-

tion trend is losing its resilience in the influencer crowd because it's been over-done in the last 5 years. These companies use the same artists, and people see right through it. As an artist, you either accept those facts and work with them, or you don't work with a corporation.

RM: What kind of integrity issues need to be addressed in the collaboration?

MH: Both the artist and the corporation need to be responsible, business-like, understanding, and all that. They need to over-communicate with each other, because their worlds are so different. It takes a lot of time and energy to get things done in a corporate environment, because a corporation is a huge team that is constantly building consensus. Decisions take longer than they do for the artist who does everything for (him/her)self, for the most part. Communication, I think, is the best way to overcome some of the integrity issues in the project. Both parties really need to do some groundwork before getting involved with one other. Fundamentally, it is a business relationship, and that background work is important. It needs to be copasetic. Does each party agree with the other's actions? History? Reputation? Products/art? PR? Both parties have a lot to lose here. The corporation could wind up being undermined by the artist's work and not know it. The corporation could saturate the market with advertising about a product without the artist knowing it. For the corporation, they need to really ask themselves what they're trying to get and why. Why are they approaching an artist or someone to tell their story for them? Does that make sense with their overall marketing plan and image? Are they being honest with their brand? Are they undermining their brand's authenticity by jumping on a trend for a quick fix? People are skeptical when a corporation's narrative is not simply about their product and their product's design.

RM: That's right. A lot of times, "brand extensions" don't equate to "product extensions." If a company's role is going to be more involved than behind-the-scenes patronly support, then you have to ask yourself, "Why does this company want to get into the art business?"

MH: And corporations have always sponsored art shows. What integrity issues are at play in those situations? Does it ultimately depend on how present the sponsor's logo is? Does it depend on how "distinguished" the artist is? I've noticed a lot of recent shows at the Guggenheim have been sponsored by Delta Airlines. I'm not too sure what an airline has to do with art, except that most of us have to fly to NY to peep Matthew Barney at the Guggenheim. There's not a lot of government funding of the arts, so it makes sense that the corporations are stepping up to the plate. As long as the message doesn't get tangled, or as long as the entanglement is mutual—like with your *Sponsorship* show in Los Angeles or like that Takashi Murakami vs. Yves St. Laurent show.

RM: What are the integrity issues that need to be addressed with the artists?

MH: From the artist's standpoint, the first question I think they really need to ask is, "How does this relate to my work? Is it a natural extension of what I do? Or is this corporation going to bastardize and commodify what is from my soul?" It's the same on the corporation's side. I think if the product is too much of a stretch from what you normally do, then it's too much of a stretch.

RM: Exactly, the relationship and subsequent product or object needs to be organically formed. What do you suggest doing to ensure that a relationship with a corporation fosters that organic growth?

MH: Follow the phrase, "It's not what you deserve, it's what you negotiate." Artists need to be real and put all of their questions and concerns on the table. It's all going to affect your work, your reputation, and consequently, your future. And know that there are always purists out there who will attack fine artists who cross the line.

RM: Often those attacks are based on generational prejudices. You made a great point earlier about recognizing that this is all simply a reflection of the world that these artists grew up in and are now a part of. But what about the wack projects that you've seen?

MH: Frankly, I've seen a lot of collaborations between companies and artists, and I just don't understand why some of them happened. The end-product didn't relate to either party's work. For this reason, I would also hope that the corporations would involve the artist in the formation of the idea of the project from the beginning— not just call up artists to decorate the products they make. We've seen a lot of those: art cars, watches, footbeds, soccer balls, perfume bottles, you name it. I think what's going on here with most of the collaborations is more in the realm of design than fine art. It all begs the question, "Is this stuff really art?"

Rich Jacobs

A Southern California–transplant living in Brooklyn, Rich Jacobs is an artist and curator whose work is shown internationally. He curates the ongoing Move *series of group exhibitions and plans to publish a series of art books. (newimageartgallery.com and galaxia-platform.com)*

RM: Tell me about some of the projects you've been involved in.

RJ: As far as projects that have been with companies, I've done some design work for X-Large.

RM: How did that come about?

RJ: It's kind of weird. How it came about is I had a show at New Image in Los Angeles, and this woman that I know came to the show and took digital photos of my work and pitched it to her boss at X-Large, who, as it turns out, was already familiar with my work from having seen an earlier show.

RM: What was that project all about?

RJ: I designed a pattern that went on a skirt and a woman's coat. It was the first time I had ever done clothing stuff.

RM: Was it labeled "Rich Jacobs for X Large?"

RJ: Kind of like that, yeah. And I designed the hang tags and all that stuff. They were more open to that, and then on their web site, they had this little feature. It was actually kind of sensitive to the artist instead of just stealing.

RM: So, they were helping to educate people about you as an artist and your work?

RJ: Right, which I appreciated. I think that's a good way look at it. That was my first experience.

RM: And that was a few years ago?

RJ: Yeah, about two years ago. Since then, I've been doing some stuff for this Japanese company that has a store here in Manhattan. They asked me to do something for the men's line. It's like the casual, almost hip-hop Japanese clothing line thing, and it's pretty low-key, not over the top fashion and stuff, you know? It's just like coats, stuff like that. So, I designed a parka.

RM: Because of their approach you felt like it

was a good match, because it wasn't over the top and too loud?

RJ: Yeah, and I trusted them as people. I got to know them first a little bit and saw how they reacted to what I was doing. I guess the fact that some friends had worked with them helped me trust them a little more. You know, you can't just do things because your friends are doing it, but it helps to know that you have someone that you can ask a question and get an honest answer. I felt comfortable, and it's actually been a good situation. I've been doing t-shirt designs and textiles and things for them for a little while. I'm having fun doing it, and it's something that just kind-of happened.

RM: It's rewarding financially?

RJ: Sure, and they're good people. I trust them. They're nice, and it's not a huge operation. They only have one store in America that sells it. There are quite a few stores in Japan that I think have it, but it's pretty low-key I would say. I feel comfortable with that kind of thing: People who are trying to do their own thing and just incorporate artists to help them realize their vision.

RM: Because you're on such good terms with them you don't worry about them producing more than they say they do or manipulating your work?

RJ: Yeah, but that sort of thing does happen, even on a small level, you know what I mean?

RM: All the more reason to get things in writing and get contracts?

RJ: Yeah, and I've learned to carefully word my invoices, like "this is being used for this," but it still happens. So you've got to watch out. It's not like small companies are any more honest.

"I keep thinking of that RUN DMC lyric that goes, 'Calvin Klein's no friend of mine, don't want nobody's name on my behind.'"

Rich Jacobs

Hopefully you can go to the source of the problem if there is one. If you live close by, you can deal with it a little easier. I've always been a little bit skeptical of commercial reasons for having art involved. If it's not something that you can trust, it feels weird.

RM: How do you handle when people approach you wanting to work with you?

RJ: I don't want to make it sound like that's happened a lot, but it has happened a little bit—more probably for curatorial reasons like, "Oh, we heard you do this or…" you can kind-of tell when people want something. It's hard, because you don't want to be just outright mean to people, but you want to guard your own opinions and things that are dear to you.

RM: Especially in the role of curator, you want to guard the people that you're curating?

RJ: Yeah, exactly. It's not like you want to just be throwing people out there to get manipulated.

RM: Does your role as curator put you in a precarious situation?

RJ: Yeah, it's tough on that level, because people aren't as sensitive in certain realms about people's privacy. For example, they call up and ask me for someone who's popular at the time's phone number, and I'm like, "Wait, I don't know if they want me giving that out. Let me ask them first." But then again, I don't want to blow opportunities for them by not giving them the message. You always want to make sure that people…

RM: Respect their privacy?

RJ: Yeah. They don't want to be hassled by people who are just going to be giving them a hard time anyway. That's a hard thing to balance as a curator, or gallery owner, or magazine person or,

you know, people who know that you know the people you know.

RM: In addition to protecting other people, how do you protect yourself? How do you say no?

RJ: That's a tough question. I'm not very good at it yet. I'm learning to be more creative in the way I say no. I'm trying to figure that out as I go, and I think the best way is to just tell people, "I appreciate you asking me…It's nice of you…The fact that you're considering me is flattering, but I don't feel comfortable with your product or your policies…" You can say, "I'm a little bit busy right now, and this is something that I may not really be interested in even if I wasn't busy, because I don't like the fact that you own sweatshops." Things like that.

RM: A lot of artist aren't interested in a company's policy, but it matters to you?

RJ: Yeah, I mean, it matters somewhat to me. I'm not going to pretend like I know everyone's background. If there are things that are real obvious, like the way a company treats their employees, you can't just pretend like it's not happening because you need money. You have to live with your own conscience. I feel like if people make decisions to work for big companies, I don't hold it against them. I have good friends who do work all the time for big corporations.

RM: Has there ever been an instance where you changed your opinion about an artist because of their association with a company?

RJ: When I was younger, there were more examples of that, when I really held dear to me these ideals about punk rock. Then these bands would jump to a big label and I'd be like, "Wait, what are you doing?" That kind of thing. I saw a lot of it happen, and I was kind of in the middle of the road on it, to be honest. I never would go out there and boycott. I think it's kind-of ridiculous.

RM: We've spoken before about the difference between being young and idealistic and then realizing when your older the realities of paying rent.

RJ: Sure yeah, that's an issue. It's all a little bit trickier when you get older—when you're just trying to survive, trying to pay rent. When you're younger, you work at a fast food place or something, obviously you may not be totally behind it, but you want to have gas money for your car. People do rationalize things, and I think holding on to some of that youthful idealism is not a bad idea. I guess it's a bad set-up, but it's reality, so that's how it works.

RM: It's a reality because there aren't a lot of other options.

RJ: There are not a lot of other options, and that's unfortunate.

RM: Maybe these corporations are the last hope for artists in general?

RJ: If there's a way to use their money—if they're interested in really helping the situation—then it shouldn't be an advertisement.

RM: Let's talk about some of your other projects.

RJ: A lot of the shows that I've curated haven't really been sponsored. They've been just straight gallery shows through the gallery. There have been a few exceptions to that. Like, I helped co-curate a show in Philadelphia that was the original skateboard show with John Freeborn. He used to run a space there called One Pixel, where I had shown a few times. He was working with 222 Gallery and asked if I could help them get some of my friends in. I felt OK with that, because I trusted John.

And I'm not mad at John for doing this, but I didn't really know about the back of the catalog which said, "Urban Outfitters and Strength Magazine." I didn't know that, and as it turns out, I think they didn't even end up paying anything. It's just like they got their logos on there, and they didn't even contribute.

RM: What's the story behind that?

RJ: I guess they had promised some money and didn't come through with it maybe, so they ended up winning on that level. I don't think anyone really knew about it too much. It didn't seem like everyone was upfront about it. And then Taka kind-of took that show to Japan and pretty much changed the entire roster of artists. And at the last minute, he told me that Nike was involved with printing the catalog.

RM: Yeah, I wasn't told about that either until after the fact.

RJ: Yeah, definitely. You know, I think I'd made the boards already, and he was like, "Well, Nike's going to pay for the catalog." I think I had already given him the boards.

RM: I felt like it soured the exhibition. It tainted it to a degree. It was very sneaky, and a lot of artists felt screwed.

RJ: I have to say that I didn't know that until it was kind-of too late. I keep thinking of that RUN DMC lyric that goes, "Calvin Klein's no friend of mine, don't want nobody's name on my behind." It seems like this kind of thing is happening more and more often, and maybe it means that artists have to ask harder questions without seeming like an ass. You have to ask people, "Who is sponsoring this show?" You don't think you need to be wondering about that. Maybe it's something that you have to think about more now.

RM: We'll start seeing anti-sponsorship clauses.

RJ: Sure, I think so, because—not to talk trash on Taka or people who have been using this kind of thing—but I think everyone would appreciate more upfrontness about it. It's really funny, because these companies don't seem to mind having the association with these artists who don't even like them. It's not about the artists. It's not about even the art. For whatever reason, these artists have been considered cool or fashionable or popular, so it's about capturing that essence. I don't even feel like they know what the art is about, or they don't even care. For example, in that skateboard show, Chris Johanson's piece? It was making fun of the whole issue. I was pretty psyched when I saw that. It seems funny, because these companies don't seem to be aware that most people don't want to be associated with them—it's not even a concept they can comprehend. I don't know why, but it seems like a few companies in particular… and not just to name names or point fingers, but when I lived in Los Angeles, it seemed like Levi's was really aggressive about trying to sponsor shows. And there are a few companies like Red Bull. You go to any opening and there are Red Bull drinks free everywhere. I don't know what Red Bull is exactly, but I don't know what it and art have to do with each other. Maybe there is some connection that I don't know about.

RM: What happened at the 222 Gallery show and the Gallery Rocket skateboard show in Japan almost parallels what happened with the Royal Elastics show in London last year that we were both in.

RJ: Yeah, that was confusing too. I didn't even know what Royal Elastics really was until I saw that catalog and there were all these shoe ads in the catalog.

RM: Right. Next to the work there were ads that mimicked the work.

RJ: You're like, "What is this?" I can honestly say that I was told that our flights were going to be paid for. But I ended up not getting that, and I had to pay for my own ticket and then… it just ended up being this big weird thing. I honestly think that the person who put on that show had good intentions, and then maybe due to not being super-responsible with sharing information at the right time…I don't know. I felt like it was a bit misleading. I was grateful to be in the show. There's another issue that is somewhat related and confusing as well. That show was called "Streetwise," and it's kind of like making something that could be marketable to these companies that may not even be an accurate reflection of what the work is really all about.

RM: Yeah, it sure felt like that shit was packaged and pitched before it was even curated.

RJ: Right! For example, I know that some artists, like me and you perhaps even moreso than some of the other artists, don't consider themselves to be "street artists." Not to diss it, but I just felt like the message is getting pretty mixed, and maybe the reason why it was called that was so Royal Elastics could get behind it. I guess it'd be nice to think that people are looking at your art for that reason alone—because they want to look at your art, and not because you're a "street artist" or you wear Royal Elastics or whatever. I don't want to seem ungrateful and complain about everything. I respect the way other people do their shows and set up their curation, but I guess it would be nice if people would be a little bit more responsible and sensitive to what the artists are really all about and not try to lump them into a category that they might not even have anything to do with. Ultimately, the artist has to take control of his own position and not seem helpless about it. Do you really want to be helping Nike advertise? If you do, then that's fine, just do it.

RM: These artist are assuming a powerless role.

RJ: And that's what makes them powerless—by thinking they are. I feel like probably most people would be happier without the association. At least that's what I've found in the dealings that I've had with artists as a curator.

RM: What about artists co-branding themselves with companies in the pursuit of making limited-edition t-shirts or skateboards, or figures? What the hell does "limited-edition" really mean any-more?

RJ: It's just a sales phrase at this point—limited in the amount that they pay the artist! I've done a few t-shirt designs here and there, and I haven't made an action figure or any of that kind of thing. I just try to take projects on that I think will be fun. If it feels right, if it feels like something that I can relate to or people that I care about could relate to, then I use that as a barome-ter. Sometimes I'm up for a challenge, like with that women's clothing thing I designed. I don't wear women's clothing, but it was kind-of like, well, I've never done that, and I want to see what that's like. And I tried it out, and it was fun. It was a fun project.

RM: Do you hope that a lot of people see your work, regardless of what format it's in?

RJ: I'm definitely not opposed to it. I guess I'm kind-of shy, and I've never made work with that specific intention. I'd rather see what happens than predict it or force it in areas. I don't make it in total isolation. It's not so private that I can't share it, but I'm not really motivated a whole lot about forcing people to see my work. I make a lot of work that doesn't get seen—a lot of it is pretty experimental and just little tests for myself. I take photos, and I don't think I've ever had a show of my photo work.

RM: As a curator, what would you look for in a relationship with a company sponsor?

RJ: I can't really think of a company that I'd want to be a sponsor for an art show that I did. Maybe for something that I needed.

RM: Like an alcohol sponsor?

RJ: I don't actually drink, so that wouldn't even help me out too much. My preference would be for a smaller company that I could relate to or could see myself buying their product—someone that I could trust, someone that I felt was coming to it from an appreciation level, someone that could give something back to the community instead of just taking from it. I do things as cheaply as possible and sort-of hope that people understand that I don't have a huge budget. In all the shows that I've ever created, I can't think of one where I've actually done a full-color invite. And I'm not bragging about that or saying it's any better, I just haven't had the money to really do more than that.

RM: If you did, would you do things differently?

RJ: That's a good question. I guess if money were no object, there would probably be more experi-mentation, and there probably would end up being more possibilities. So, I'm not opposed to that kind of thing. I just haven't had the opportunity. For me, I'm always hopeful that the artwork itself was what would convince people to want to check out a show. That's not to say you don't have any responsibility to help people know about it as a curator, but I feel like the work should be selling the show, not the sponsors. I hope that people go look at art because they're interested in art. I feel like the message can get out in a simple way. That's just my approach. Some people might have a hard time with that, want something more fancy, and I understand that. I do. I just have tried to keep it pretty basic and simple that way.

RM: Are there examples of companies that were around back in the day and were supportive and grew with the artists?

RJ: I don't know all my facts on this, but it seems like, and I don't even know what Agnés B. is, but I know it's a clothing fashion thing, and I can remember their name being around in the early graffiti days and that she helped a lot of artists. I feel like there are companies that have championed creativity and helped artists to get out there more, and that's not a bad thing. It seems like when we were in London, Ro-Starr was over there painting a mural in her store. She was willing to let him do that and pay him to do that. She was simply having a mural in her store. To me, I can back that. I think that's admirable. It shows a level of appreciation and understanding rather than manipulation. I hope there can be more of that.

RM: Can you imagine a big company saying, "Yes we'll support the show, and by the way, don't tell anyone?"

RJ: I always was appreciative of that magazine called *Super X*. It existed for a short time in Japan. My understanding is that it was backed by Casio. They were the ones who were paying for that, and I think maybe there was one Casio ad in the whole magazine. Basically they allowed the curator of the magazine to do whatever he wanted. To me, that's a neat example. Their whole trip was sort-of like creating this new form of media, because basically they weren't charging for the magazine. They were just distributing all over the country and world. Casio paid for it to be printed, but they weren't being super-overt about it.

RM: It seems like that Casio project is a good model.

RJ: It was pretty smart, and I think there are companies out there willing to recognize what makes certain aspects of culture interesting and fun for people. Culture happens in spite of big companies, and it happens because it's part of life. It happens because people are out there doing things, and they're not being controlled by companies while they're doing it. I wish more companies could realize that fact, and just let people be human and let culture flourish.

"I've seen weird bootlegs of my stuff before… of t-shirts and stuff like that. If I can find stuff like that, I buy it. I think it's fine. That's cool."

TODD JAMES (REAS)

Todd James

Todd James (REAS) is an artist who lives and works in New York and Los Angeles.

RM: How do you decide which companies to work with?

TJ: Well, you just have to gauge it according to what your interests are. If you like a certain company that might approach you, or if the deal that they're bringing to you is a really good one mutually, then I think it's great. There are a bunch of different reasons why I might not do something— if I don't like the particular direction the brand is moving in at the time, or if they're doing something that I'm not in tune with, or if what they're doing behind the scenes is weird. I think as long as a corporation is funding art, as long as they're not completely taking advantage of the artist, and they say, "Here's money for the project. Go do what you want with it. If we sell it, we'd like to make our costs back," then that's cool. But when they say, "Hey, guess what? We want to use you and give you nothing and then gain some credibility," then that's not cool. Those are the companies that I choose not to work with.

RM: Often the real agenda is hidden.

TJ: Yeah, maybe the artists don't know at the time that that's the way it's going to turn out. Maybe it's presented one way, and it turns into something else later. Sometimes I think it's not even about the art. It's about what they think the art or the artist represents. They want to attach themselves to that as a way to reach youth culture, popular culture, subculture, or whatever.

RM: That Altoids project you told me about is a good example of that.

TJ: Yeah, I just don't think that was a hundred percent on the up-and-up. From what I understood, they paid an artist $1,500 to create a billboard-sized piece of artwork, and then they kept the original artwork. I don't know how much an agency would charge somebody to design and layout the type for an ad that big, but I have a feeling it would be more than that.

RM: You originally turned down that project?

TJ: Yeah. They said up front what they were going to do, and I just didn't think that it was worth it. I don't know enough to say how it worked, but I know that the artist was given $1,500 for something that Altoids could keep. I mean, even if you're buying the art...come on.

RM: Are there projects that you've taken on that have worked out well?

TJ: Yeah, well, Sakura International did a huge art week, "Untitled 2000," in Japan. They brought all these different artists over from America to do this thing, and each person had their own space to exhibit their work. It was a serious thing. It was well done, and everybody was taken care of. Anything that we needed that was within the realm of possibility, they would make happen. So, I thought that was a good example.

RM: What products came out of that?

TJ: There were a bunch of t-shirts and skateboards that everybody did that went along with it. Again, everybody was paid really well, and they were limited-edition shirts, and they didn't edit the work. They were just like, yeah cool-cool-cool check-check-check.

RM: Any other companies that you've worked with? What about that Puma project?

TJ: That was presented as a cool soccer project that was supposed to tie in directly to the World Cup. It was pretty basic, and it was pretty easy. I think Puma got involved after the fact. I think during the course of the project, the organizers found Puma as their sponsor. I don't know. That was weird, too. I don't even know how it ended up. I only know that I did a soccer ball and a jersey. That's where it ended. It wasn't that big a deal to me.

RM: You know, they're taking your stuff and blowing it up and using it at these shows.

TJ: Well, yeah, that's a little weird, but whatever. I'm not gonna, you know, freak out about it. I don't really care. Weird shit just happens.

RM: When something doesn't go as planned, does it prevent you from working with them in the future?

TJ: Oh, absolutely yeah! I don't think I'll be doing anything with them again.

RM: Has your opinion of an artist ever changed because of a company they've worked with, or decisions they've made?

TJ: Knowing how it all works, unless somebody continuously makes bad decisions, that usually doesn't bother me. I haven't really seen too much of it. I just either like what you're doing or I don't. It doesn't matter. I don't really mind if somebody's all over the map. Like, they did this thing with this company and that thing with that company—as long as I like what they're making, it doesn't bother me that much. This is a capitalist society, and I don't have any problems with capitalism. I just think that if you're making a deal with somebody, it should be an honest one.

RM: You've been successful with producing and distributing things yourself.

TJ: Yeah, but some of those shirts I've done with other companies like Sakura, and it works out fine. Other times, I do stuff with other companies. You know, you still get other fair deals or whatever, but the books and stuff, that's really more my work. I'd rather keep control of that. If the right book company wanted to do something, then I'd definitely consider it. I also like the idea of just doing it myself. You know, you've got your books and other products that you make. A lot of people that we know do their own product production. So, I think it's good. I think that's the best thing.

RM: I agree. I think this is a reflection of the DIY mindset we grew up in, and that carries over to your work with Funny Garbage and Crank Yankers. You are now in a position where you can make your own television show. Do you see your work on Crank Yankers as something that's separate from all the art stuff?

TJ: No. I mean, it's separate, but, you know, you can still see that I've done it. There are a lot of elements in there from other things that I've done. They all cross over—the commercial work and the gallery work cross over and intersect—the way it looks or the attitude of it, or whatever. Crank Yankers is an odd project, because there are really very few boundaries as to what we can do on the show. I'm not edited. There are no real guidelines. I don't want to give examples, because it's just too weird, but there's no rhyme or reason. And it's all pretty outrageous. If I were working on the Smurfs, it would be different, because it would really be like a job. It wouldn't be like I'm working and we're creating something, because there'd be so many boundaries put up. For example, "He has to be blue," and, "You can't curse on the Smurfs!" You can curse on Crank Yankers. We can make them naked. We can do anything. So we have no boundaries.

RM: As far as authorship and the identity you attach to your work, what is the difference between REAS and Todd James?

TJ: Well REAS is a thing I did in the past, but I still use the word in my work. As far as me feeling the name is my identity,…it's less now than it was when I was a teenager. It's part of my history. I think fewer and fewer people call me by that now.

RM: Any opinions on different projects that you've seen?

TJ: You know what I think is cool? Bad bootlegging. I don't know how it fits in, but I like when something is poorly bootlegged. It's off model, but it's the imitation of a product or a thing, and it's totally like a knock-off.

RM: Or an artist's product? Like KAWS dolls.

TJ: Well, yeah, that would be more of what I'm thinking about. Like if it wasn't exactly copied. Like it's something else. It's kind-of like when they do The Flintstones, but on the t-shirt they make Fred's jacket green and his skin is pink, and Barney's wearing a red shirt and it's printed in Mexico.

RM: Has that happened with your work?

TJ: I've seen weird bootlegs of my stuff before… of t-shirts and stuff like that. If I can find stuff like that, I buy it. I think it's fine. That's cool.

RM: Would you consider doing a video game?

TJ: Absolutely. Without a doubt.

RM: Would you wait to be approached, or would you pitch your own idea?

TJ: Both, but I don't have the time to pitch. A game is such a daunting idea, because it involves materials and programmers and things that I really don't know much about. Programming? Wow, holy shit—to do what they're doing on this level?

It's like a movie production or something so, I don't know. But I know other people who have made games. Like, Rodney Allan Greenblatt with Parrapa the Rapper. I love that, I think that's great. I'd love to do something like that. I just haven't thought about it. I mean, I've thought about it, but I just haven't really put it into action—whatever that would be. I haven't thought about how I would participate or what I would do.

RM: That's why Crank Yankers is such a good match.

TJ: Yeah totally. Those video games are more like…I'm kind-of admiring the stuff, you know? Like these mechanical robots—stuff that I'm into that's outside of everything else.

RM: Rodney Allan Greenblatt made that shift from fine art?

TJ: I think he still does both. I really don't know that much about what he does, but yeah, I think he made the big switch. I think Sony just loves him, and those people just love his work. I think they pitched him the idea for the game. I'm not sure, but I think they did. I think he faxed them over some drawings and they told him to just go with it.

RM: So, Sony is a patron of sorts for his work. Or can Parrapa the Rapper not be considered "his work" anymore?

TJ: I don't know. I don't really know how it works. I think we're younger, and we see things differently. We like Banana Splits and Saturday-morning cartoons the same way we like some things in a gallery. I think some things are definitely on the same level. You just gotta pick and choose from each world you know.

Like, what's highest on your list of things that you like? I think that's how I look at things. I love HR Puff-N-Stuff, and I love Basquiat. I like that the same level of artistry and talent went into making both things—maybe not the same attitude or world, but it doesn't matter. Just like with this game here. This game is fucking insane. The whole production is insane. You've got your blockbusters, and then you've got your films.

RM: But I also think it's risky when companies use artists as a sales strategy.

TJ: Yeah, I guess so. You just gotta decide what you like and what you don't like. As long as they let you do stuff you want to do.

RM: And that's what I mean—assuming a role where there is a "they" who let or don't let you do things. But a lot of the artists really need the money.

TJ: I hear that. That's true.

Chris Johanson

Chris Johanson is an artist who lives and works in San Francisco. He has exhibited his work internationally and was included in the 2002 Whitney Biennial.

RM: Have you been involved in any projects that have been corporate sponsored?

CJ: Well, I've been in group shows that were sponsored. I'm sure every non-profit show that I've ever been in was sponsored by a corporation. Personally, I think it should be a law that corporations contribute to the arts and to education. It should be mandatory. And it shouldn't even be that they get brownie points or anything. It should be part of local government allowing a company to do business in their city. That should just be part of it.

RM: Some of these sponsored events almost turn into advertising vehicles and others are more low-key.

CJ: Yeah. There's a range—like some corporate stadium, which is the blatant, over-the-top example. It's really gross to me that all these auditoriums and stadiums are named after corporations. To me, it's just a sign of really grotesque times.

RM: It could end up backfiring on them. Perhaps people won't want to go to the Staples Center.

CJ: They'd rather go to something that has a history than some pre-fab weird new mega-plex that they probably underpaid everybody involved in to make happen.

RM: In some cases, corporations create artificial histories and stories in order to make these places seem more authentic.

CJ: Yeah, and they staff the place with whatever the minority is of the area and try to pay them totally shitty wages. They probably don't let them unionize, and…and I should qualify first that I have had a corporation sponsor a solo show of mine.

RM: What does that mean?

CJ: What that meant was that we had this private party and,…I don't want to say the company's name, because I just don't. But they were, like, so outer-space from where I was coming from anyway. I feel that it was an interesting thing to do, but I'll never do it again—you know, have a sponsor. Anyway, they sponsored this private party, which was a fun party, and they made these t-shirts. They gave me all these t-shirts, and then I silkscreened on them "VA" for Vampirism Anonymous. And then it had kind-of a personal account of how Vampires Anonymous had helped this individual.

RM: Why did this company want to be involved in the show?

CJ: I guess to be hip or whatever, and then I went ahead and purposefully and obnoxiously made a shirt that was against them.

RM: Did you solicit their involvement in the beginning?

CJ: No. The gallery asked me, and I was so busy preparing for the show that I didn't really think about it. Then I realized that, even though I made this shirt, which was, in effect, a critique against what was happening, I personally don't feel comfortable with corporate sponsorship at all.

RM: That's a unique way of turning it back around on itself.

CJ: Yeah. It did come off, but the thing is, I could have avoided the whole thing by just saying no—which is my stance now. I just don't feel like I want to be involved with any of those companies on any level. I also think skateboarding companies are different for me, because I only do skateboard graphics occasionally, and when I do, it's for a company that I really respect or it's for a

"I've been cutting off the logos on my shoes. I've just been cutting them out, and I'm not buying new shoes. I've just been going to thrift stores, and getting rid of the logos, because that's the last thing I want to be. I just don't want to be a part of any of that shit."

Chris Johanson

rider whom I respect. The main case in point is Anti-Hero. I just think that they're very cool in their politics, and I think they try to make graphics that are really punk and question the status quo. They do stuff like (and I didn't make this particular one but I'll give you an example) that says, "McJesus, over two billion killed," and I think that's such a good board. It fucks with people, and it's issue-oriented. I think that's good art. I'm just not interested in ever doing a shoe for anybody or being involved in any of that stuff. I understand why a lot of people I know are, but I was never a pro skateboarder, and I was never an amateur skateboarder. So I never came up in that, and I never needed to get sponsors to keep doing my thing. But to be a pro skater and to go traveling, you need all your sponsors and stuff, I guess. I really don't know much about it.

RM: Money is coming from corporations because government grants have dried up. There are not many opportunities for an artist to get untainted money.

CJ: Untainted money, yeah. It's hard to even figure out what that is, huh?

RM: How have you been able to solve that dilemma?

CJ: Well, I've always just lived really cheap. I'll go back to talking about how I didn't come from the skateboard industry, and I didn't come from the surfing industry, or whatever. I don't even know what that means, but I'm sure it's like the same thing. I didn't come from those places and then get into art. And also I didn't come from a graphic design background. When you go to graphic design school, from my little experience with it, you learn about having a business sense

and all that.

RM: From my experience, the work tends to be business and commerce-driven.

CJ: Exactly, and I didn't come from there, and I didn't come from the graffiti background—which is like the whole scamming shit from people routine and ripping shit off, and all that. It's all like, you know, racking all your paint and getting over. Again, I don't know much about that lifestyle, but I do know that there is a certain scam-factor that goes with it. And see, I didn't come from any of those backgrounds, so I didn't really have that to develop into my work and the way I feel about art and commerce.

RM: The graffiti-informed model seems to be to try to turn the tables so you're not getting fucked. Corporations are staking claim to public spaces, and graff artists are taking it back.

CJ: There's a certain "get over" on people aspect to that stuff that I've noticed and witnessed. And to get back to this art and commerce stuff…you know, I just moved to San Francisco when I was twenty, and I went to school and stuff a little, and I just always had a job. I'm from San José, and I always had a job. So, I don't know, I guess it's the way my parents raised me—work and try to make your own way.

RM: There must be some delineation between the work that's done to pay your rent and the work that you're doing on canvases or whatever.

CJ: Well, I painted houses professionally. I got into the trade, and I would scam paint from job sites and wood from job sites. Basically, I've been just like a housepainter forever. I never really thought about professional pursuits as an artist. I seriously just found myself in this situation.

When opportunities presented themselves, I took them. Like when Aaron (Rose) said, "Do you want to come do a show in New York?" I definitely said yeah, and I stepped up to the plate. For any opportunities that anybody's given me, I've fully dealt with my side of the bargain.

RM: Because that was the direction you wanted to go in?

CJ: Exactly. Maybe you could say it was conservative, but I just kind-of felt more comfortable with identifying myself just as somebody who had a job and not as a visual artist. And then I've just found myself in this situation now, where I'm not a housepainter. I'm actually surviving off my paintings.

RM: Which is a real accomplishment.

CJ: Yeah, it's really rare. I'm lucky.

RM: Well, I wouldn't say "lucky" per se. There were opportunities that presented themselves that you seized in order to go in a direction that you wanted to go in, and that's all on top of making good work.

CJ: I have people asking me, and I've thought about working with this person or that person, and I've had to think about all this stuff—corporations and stuff. What I basically came up with is that I'm just not interested. A cigarette company a while ago wanted me to do a mural, and I said fuck no. I mean, that didn't take long to think about at all.

RM: What are some of the ones that you had to think more seriously about?

CJ: There were some clothing companies. See, the thing with the t-shirt companies in Japan is, to me, that's so harmless. If anything, I'm getting ripped off majorly, but I don't really care. It's just

so funny to make a t-shirt. A lot of times the shirt designs that I give are just so ridiculous that it's just fun to see if somebody would even wear something so ridiculous, you know what I mean? And that was just fun and games, and really, in the end, it's just a t-shirt. It's not like doing a t-shirt for Shell or doing a t-shirt for Nike or whatever.

RM: But it is for someone's brand, in some ways.

CJ: Yeah, but with these last people that I'm working with, 2K,—I just think they're nice people. I mean, it's just some dudes that have families. The people that I work with on prints, the Paulsen Press people, it's like a woman-owned company, and they have families. They're just down-to-earth and grass-roots. I mean, I totally understand why my friends who make movies do commercials. They're saving money to make these epics. A lot of times, you have to invest your own money in your things, and I can understand those kinds of decisions. I just don't relate personally with my work, so I never want to work for anybody. When you paint somebody's house, it's just so mellow. You're not hurting anybody. You're not selling culture. I'm not interested in these shoe companies that pay people shit wages and then come back here and hire some sexy teenager skateboarder, and pay them a hundred thousand dollars. I think it's totally grotesque. I'm totally against it, and I don't want anything to do with those people. And they want to endorse the art shows, you know. They want to be hip. That's all they're doing. They're really trying to be hip.

RM: And where were they eight years ago?

CJ: Yeah, I don't understand it. I'm so unagitated about this stuff, really. But I know that nine out of ten times, it seems like with anything corporate, it means that they're burning people super hardcore to get ahead. Every time I hear a story about a corporation, it's usually negative. Like, they get some hip photographer to shoot their ad, and pay them as little as possible, and as soon as they get the photographs, they just try not to pay the person period. And then end up paying the photographer maybe six months later. It's just obvious that they're evil scammers.

RM: Has your opinion of an artist or a company ever changed because of some project that they've done?

CJ: Yeah definitely. I think you're tainting your work. I mean, I understand mixing it up if, like somebody's an illustrator, or whatever. I understand that's how you've chosen to make your money, but I think it's really interesting when fine art hits that.

RM: You'd hope that art isn't watered down by someone else's agenda?

CJ: Yeah, you'd hope. It's a complicated world, and everybody's got their own trip. The truth is the fucking assholes that run these big companies—they can just tell their people to change your art thirty percent, and then they can do whatever they want with it anyways. In some situations, people I know have been told, "This person I worked with got the orders to change your art this percentage so that it could fly."

RM: Change someone's artwork in order to use it legally without the artist's permission?

CJ: Yeah. They saw this person's art in a magazine, and they changed it thirty percent. That's what these fashion companies do. That's the law, and so that's what they do. They don't want to

think for themselves. They don't want to come up with their own ideas. They just want to suck people's individual creativity and homogenize it.

RM: And then there's no longer an individual behind the work, but rather, an anonymous corporation.

CJ: They don't need to do that. They don't need to take somebody's individual art that they've been working on for the last five years to make their point. They don't need to take that person's art and do that. I hate it all so much that I try not to even buy anything anymore.

RM: It's becoming increasingly difficult to buy anything that you'd be proud to own. I'm at the point where I try not to wear anyone's name on my clothes.

CJ: Me too. I've been cutting off the logos on my shoes. I've just been cutting them out, and I'm not buying new shoes. I've just been going to thrift stores and getting rid of the logos, because that's the last thing I want to be. I just don't want to be a part of any of that shit.

RM: A lot of artists are self-producing lower-priced items to get their work out to a more mainstream audience. Is that one of the reasons that you've done t-shirts in the past?

CJ: That's the one thing that I can say is from coming up through punk and being a punk-rock teenager. I always made skateboard-zines or art-zines and always made editions of things, and I always liked to give people stuff—CDs and zines. My drawings are still cheap, you know what I mean? I do big paintings now that cost a lot of money, I guess, but I'm thirty-four now, and I waited a long time to like...

RM: Until you had to push them up?

CJ: Yeah. I know a lot of people whose prices went up, and they wanted that. And I know a lot of people who have kept their prices low, because they thought it was the right thing to do, and I'm one of them. I just didn't want to be involved in an economy that was only for rich people, and that's why I still have drawings that are cheap. That's why I make a lot of art, and that's why I do lots of editions, t-shirts, buttons, and ephemera. Right now I'm looking across the room at a Raymond Pettibon. Pettibons from the eighties, regardless of what he wanted to do, go for a lot of money. They're thousands of dollars now for a drawing. No matter what you do, stuff's going to start to be sold for a lot of money.

RM: You can't control the secondary market.

CJ: All you can do is keep selling stuff for cheap, and I think that's a good thing to do.

RM: And you can produce the work yourself.

CJ: Yeah. You can find small companies to work with, that you fully believe in.

RM: We're in a lot more empowering age now, where we can do it ourselves.

CJ: Yeah. I'm curious about these new companies that are coming up like American Apparel, for example. They seem really cool. It seems like there are a lot more people who are thinking more responsibly now, and those are the people I want to know. It doesn't have to be dog-eat-dog. You could be the person who can make the decision to either silkscreen your stuff yourself, hire your own people, or do it at a small shop that you know is a family-owned business. You can make less money at the end of the year, big deal. It just seems like the landlord always wants more money and the big business employer always wants to pay people less. It just seems like the people on top always want to figure out ways to milk the people below them.

RM: Milk them financially and culturally.

CJ: Definitely. Suck them dry. I think they should just be forced to give more to society. But really all they want to do is scam as much as they can and not be accountable for anything. That's why they have their one-eight-hundred numbers—so that you can never really talk to a human.

KAWS

KAWS is an artist who lives and works in Brooklyn, New York. (kawsone.com)

RM: What kind of corporate-sponsored projects have you worked on?

KAWS: I'm pretty careful with choosing most of the companies that I work with. There are definitely exceptions—like that show at Colette where Reebok paid for the shipping of my art to and from the gallery.

RM: And what did Reebok get?

KAWS: They got a logo that wound up being a centimeter on the invite, and they got a little logo on the front of Colette's window. It wasn't like I did any sort of work with any Reebok products or there was anything with Reebok in the show. They simply fronted the shipping costs. Colette asked me if it was okay if they sponsored, and I said that it was cool. I've worked with a lot of other companies as well. Mostly the companies that I work with I consider peers. With DC and Medicom, I feel like they're kids that I could have known when I was little. When DC approached me about doing a shoe, they were totally on. Most companies that want to do stuff automatically think in terms of "…then we can sell the key chain, and then we can make the mouse pad, and then we can…" you know? We just decided that we weren't going to do any advertising, we were only going to make a certain number, and we agreed on the fee. So, it was really a clear under-standing. It was good. I felt really comfortable working with them, because they were up-front. They put it on the table and said, "It is what it is. You can take it, or you can walk away from it, and you won't find out four months into it that suddenly it's this big project that was initially downplayed." With a company like that, I worked with them and I look forward to working with

them again. It was a good experience. They did something for me that I was interested in, that I couldn't produce on my own, because I'm not in the sneaker business. The thing was definitely very novel, but it was fun.

RM: And you only worked with the top level people there.

KAWS: Yeah, I never felt they were like, "Oh great! You're going to work with us! Here, talk to Suzy in the fucking whatever department." Honestly, I don't really have situations like that, because I don't set myself up for it. As soon as anyone mentions anything to me about doing stuff, if I consider it at all, I first really look into what they've done, with whom, and what came of it and where it went. It's a scary situation for peo-ple to work with each other if they're not on the same page. Actually, it's not scary at all—it's only making stuff. But it's kind of silly.

RM: Certainly scarier, or sillier, for you than it is for them.

KAWS: Oh yeah. The other thing is that you have other companies that approach everybody, blow threw them, and then look for another crop of fresh young artists. You know, there's no real interest in the work. They say, "Hey, you did that magazine cover. Oh you did…whatever," they're like, "Yeah we're down. We've been big fans of yours for so long."

RM: How do you say no to those companies?

KAWS: Oh I just say, "I'm working on other projects," or "I can't obligate myself to other proj-ects, because I really want to work on the stuff I'm doing now." I'm never mean. I can appreciate businesses. I have nothing against people thinking they should do what they need to do in order to

"I really feel that people should get over the taboos of commercial work. People are going to look at this book that you're doing ten years from now, and they're going to think it's silly. They'll think, 'Was this really an issue?'"

KAWS

forward their business. I just don't want to take part in it sometimes. Sometimes I can even really like the company, but the thing doesn't seem right. It doesn't seem like a good fit.

RM: What have you done with Medicom?

KAWS: First we did the Kubrick and Bearbrick stuff and then…

RM: You were already familiar with their company and products?

KAWS: Oh yeah. I've been familiar with Medicom for a few years. I always admired them. Their craftsmanship is no joke. If you're going to make a toy, you want to make it with them. They've always handled themselves well. They are a large company, and they make millions and millions of dollars on tons of stuff. It's not like they're this elitist thing, but they make most of their stuff really well. I appreciate their approach to it. That's why there are dozens of other toy companies trying to be like that company.

RM: You've worked with them on a number of projects?

KAWS: Yeah, there's the Kubrick stuff and the Bearbrick stuff. It's all sort-of the same line. For that stuff, I just licensed them my imagery.

RM: Because the molds are already there?

KAWS: There are molds, and then they do an additional sculpt for shaping. For the Kubricks, I had them make the bus shelter. For that project, they wanted to do a limited-edition KAWS project. They approached me about the idea of doing something with them for the Kubrick line, and I said, "Okay, if we can make bus shelters, I'll do it."

RM: Because that relates to your other work.

KAWS: Yeah, I mean, any project that I would

do with anybody kind-of relates to other work. It's always just another outlet for me to bend the work into different forms. In this case, I just thought the idea of little kids buying bus shelters and playing with them…the fact that most of the good things that have happened to me…all of it really started from doing those bus shelters. I just think it's a laugh—how little kids are going to fucking play with it, in their house, like all sorts of kids from all different walks of life. So, Medicom did that for me, which I could never have done on my own.

RM: You told them what you wanted, and they made it happen.

KAWS: Yeah. They were open to whatever. And then I hired them to produce another toy for me, which I completely funded. They're not backing it. I paid for the whole thing. 1,500 pieces come here, and then I sell them if I want to.

RM: I like that you're turning it around to take advantage of their facilities on your own terms.

KAWS: They oversee the production. It's great. It's just like doing a print with a really good printmaker.

RM: They're not co-branding it, like with the bus shelters?

KAWS: They still have "Produced by Medicom" or "Manufactured by Medicom" on the label. They asked, and of course, I'm like, "Yeah, sure."

RM: But they don't handle the distribution.

KAWS: Oh no. That's the difference between getting a percentage, and buying at cost and selling for retail. They'll basically still make whatever I want to make. If I want to fund it and sell it, then they'll do that, and I'll pay those fees. Or, if I want them to deal with all the costs and distribution, then they'll do that, and I'll take a royalty.

RM: What factors into making that decision?

KAWS: With the bus shelter pieces, I do want it everywhere, but I don't have those relationships. I can't make 17,000 pieces and have them go into stores and be sold all over the world. The truth is, when you do the stuff with them that they mass-produce and market, they also do all the advertising, all the PR, and all that. So, when I do produce my own stuff, usually the quantity that I make is a really small fraction compared to the stuff that we've made together. It's like they're throwing a net out for me. Then suddenly I have this thing that's really limited, and it's just supply and demand. So by letting them do that, not only am I getting really nice products made that I like, but they're building my market for me. They're doing my PR, so I never have to pay for an ad or anything. All that stuff just comes.

RM: It's also locking you into the KAWS brand.

KAWS: Well, the thing about being an individual artist is that I feel, at any point, that I could just step off. The way I see it, this is all just on the up, and I can change my mind about anything, because I'm not a corporation, and I don't have tons of employees. I'm a person in an apartment. I owe nothing to anyone. So things like that don't really stress me.

RM: How did some of your earlier projects go, like the pajamas and slippers?

KAWS: Basically all that stuff was for one season with a designer, this guy Jun Takahashi. The company is called Undercover, and he basically invited me to design stuff and license my imagery for one of his collections. It was cool, because

I have a real interest in a lot of objects. I love seeing my stuff transformed into and onto objects. It's strange, you know. You grow up, and you have these things around you, and you kind of feel this relationship to them. They come from somewhere. It's funny, because now I feel like a big little kid. It's like I'm seeing the wizard. I know where the shit's being made, and so I think when that first happens, you kind of want to do it yourself. You want to figure out a bunch of stuff and get it realized.

RM: That's what gets me pumped about actualizing products. It's empowering to demystify manufacturing processes. That knowledge fuels the creative process, and it's usually all good until the business side enters the picture. Have you had any sour experiences with companies?

KAWS: Yeah. The first toy that I made, the Companion, was totally out of my hands. I worked with a company that worked with a company that worked with a factory. I later found out that there were a lot more produced than we had agreed to make.

RM: How did that project come about?

KAWS: I was working with friends, but they were very young as well. That was the first time I saw my work in form, so I was really excited. I felt like I was doing a sculpture, but I was getting 500 of them. Honestly, at that point, I would have done it for free just to have them. The fact that they were over-run doesn't bother me financially. The only reason why it bothers me is that if I have somebody that were to buy anything that I said was limited to 500, I want it to, hands down, be 500. The integrity has to be there. I don't ever want to sell something that I'm not feeling good about, or later find out was over-produced and all over the place.

RM: Have you ever seen a situation where an artist worked for a company and it changed your opinion of the work or the artist?

KAWS: You know what? I really feel that people should get over the taboos of commercial work. People are going to look at this book that you're doing ten years from now, and they're going to think it's silly. They'll think, "Was this really an issue?" I just feel like you're not helpless.

RM: There's still this old-fashioned idea of "pure art" that people cling to.

KAWS: Which I think is such bullshit. At the end of the day—like we were talking about last time—you have this righteous fucking artist that never does any corporate anything and then, so what? Say his career goes well, and he has his show at the Whitney or wherever—all that shit is underwritten by sponsors! So his work starts going in magazines, which have advertisers. I mean, there's no difference between being in so-and-so gallery and being branded by their name. You think that doesn't carry over every time somebody sees their work? "Oh they're with da-da-da." It's like, dude, wake up! I see the world as a land of opportunity and you can run around crying and complaining, or you can make the most of the situation.

RM: When Reebok sponsored your show at Colette, would you have drawn the line at how much credit they took?

KAWS: I would if it seemed like it were over-powering the show.

RM: What if you were compensated for that presence? What's the threshold? What's the price?

KAWS: You mean if they wanted to give me like 80 Gs? I wouldn't let them turn it tacky. I would just rather pass on the money. You definitely want to maintain a level of integrity in all the work.

RM: Sometimes artists are mislabeled to appeal to a sponsor's demographic, like "street artists…"

KAWS: In almost every article, if the magazine does some Q&A with me, it's like, "Um, so how did you start your graffiti art?" Well, look at the work. Does that look like graff? Yeah, at this point, the truth is there are a lot of old people with a lot of power, and I'm really hoping that younger kids are going to grow up a bit wiser. It's already happening. You already have a lot of kids who can differentiate between fucking Wild Style, the movie, and what some kids are doing today. The thing about some of the shows that are sponsored that you were mentioning—yeah, they're trying to package these shows without really investing time and research. It's just like they obviously read it out of some magazine that misquoted a phrase. That stuff tumbles like an avalanche. All you can really do is laugh at it.

RM: How do you decide which shows to do?

KAWS: Most of the shows have been pretty straight-forward—just a space giving me a show. I did a show recently in London that was kind of sponsored. Mo Wax put it on with Gimme Five, another English company. They co-sponsored this exhibition and basically paid for everything, including flying me out. They also gave me a lot larger percentage of sales than a normal gallery would. I felt like I could enter that agreement a little more peacefully, because I've seen everything they've done. I've watched them grow. I've watched what they've done, and I like it. I like the stuff they do, and I want to do stuff with them. The integrity's always been there. The quality's always been there. One guy from Gimme Five was one of the first people to buy work from me. I think it was like '95 or whatever. He bought one of my phone ads before the idea of even selling phone ads had crossed my mind.

RM: What did they get in exchange for producing the show?

KAWS: They wanted to do it. For them it meant doing an event in London. There wasn't anything going on that they liked; they just said that they wanted to do a good show. It's good for them. It keeps them out there—not like they need to be kept out there, but I guess it's a good PR thing to present an exhibition that they feel good about to London. Before that, I didn't have an opportunity to show in London, so it wound up working for both of us.

RM: I didn't get a chance to see the show, but you never thought it was a crass presentation of your work?

KAWS: No, not at all. The space was beautiful. Honestly, I wish that galleries were like that. Although it was publically sponsored by Mo Wax, it was less of a commercial venture than a lot of galleries. There was less pressure. It was like, "Let's do something good," instead of like, "Let's sell something good." I feel separated from galleries. I just feel like I haven't really been on the same level or worked with anybody who really knows the stuff that I do or the markets that I've been playing with and the worldly grasp that this stuff has. People in the gallery world, they're just oblivious to what's going on right now. The idea of having thirty rich people be the only ones who

could see and have my work—I just wouldn't be fulfilled.

RM: As you go more mass, are you moving into the entertainment industry, or are you still delivering this thing called "art"? Or are you at the forefront of creating a new category?

KAWS: I don't ever really get caught up thinking about the category my work fits into. It spans from making limited-edition objects and it kind of grew. It's like Oldenburg on speed. My multiple editions were 25, and now they're 2,500. You take what each piece is for what it is. I have a bunch of art, and I have a bunch of toys. I look at them equally. I see stuff that I know there's 5,000 of, but if the design is awesome, I still look at it just as much as I look at that one drawing that I own. And having that stuff around in the same environment makes me question all that.

RM: It's an extension of your own tastes.

KAWS: Yeah. I mean, it all depends on who's looking. When I was little, I had my fucking Slimeball sticker or whatever stickers that I got and had to question what I stuck it on, or what board I put it on, or where I put it on that board. I'd be, like, "These are the stickers that go in the middle of the board, and these are the ones that · go under the wheels…" That stuff's precious, you know. It's those experiences that make me really want to make the stickers and make stuff that could apply like that.

RM: Those little things shouldn't be overlooked.

KAWS: Exactly. Like, "Oh this is on my cell phone. That's in my pocket every day, and I walk around with it." It's silly, but I think it means something. I think you have a lot of the same interests as far as making that sort of stuff—as far as the materials you use and…

RM: Absolutely. That's, conceptually, how our work is very similar. However, one difference I'd like to ask you about, is your use of a pseudonym. Why do you use the name KAWS?

KAWS: I always felt it was just really objective. People can look at the work without looking at the person who made it. I feel that it separates me from the work.

RM: Why do you want to do that?

KAWS: Not that I want to do that exactly, but I just don't want to get in the way of it. If I do anything in a magazine, I'd much rather have them run an image of my artwork than a picture of me. I just think a picture of me is pointless. Using "KAWS" is almost an attempt to make my work anonymous.

RM: KAWS is almost like a company brand name that takes human accountability away from the work, just like corporations do.

KAWS: I didn't really enter it conceptually like that. It kind-of came from traditional graffiti. You don't write your name because of repercussions. It's really basic. You either find a name that you like, or you find letters that you like. In my case, it was letters. I also wanted a name that wasn't a word before I used it. It kind-of just stuck, and you build it. I see everything that I make as being a part of the whole that I've been crafting.

RM: It's all part of the KAWS brand.

KAWS: Basically yeah. I feel like every artist kind-of comes off as a brand.

RM: Entire careers are built on the idea of continually creating work that is "on-brand" for an artist.

KAWS: I just honestly think that, as far as what we're doing, the smartest thing for us to do is to stop looking for handouts, because nothing's free. There's no one who cares about your work like you do. There's no one who lives with it every day like you do. I mean, it's all we've really got.

"It's going to get ugly. The people who are getting down with corporations are going to realize that these companies are not paying as much money as they should."

YOUNG KIM

Young Kim

Young Kim is a creative director and consultant whose projects continually take him around the globe. He has directed commercials and music videos for Nike, Adidas, Sony, Blockbuster, Kodak, ESPN, Sega, and VH-1 among others. He has been working on his Suit Man project for more than 10 years.

RM: We've spoken about all these companies approaching artists in order to co-brand themselves through the production of objects or events or campaigns or…whatever. What kinds of situations like these have you been involved in?

YK: I've been on both ends of the situation, as I've been in the advertising and the commercial worlds for over 15 years. Back in '91, my first project for Nike was for Phil Knight, who has a son who wanted to get into rap music. They asked that I do some underground shit.

RM: This was for Nike through Wieden and Kennedy?

YK: Yeah, but I wasn't working for Wieden and Kennedy then. I was just freelancing. So, I get this call, and they were like, "Yo, can you get us some downtown crew that's into hip hop?" I called my friend Shadi Perez and we started getting some names and people together, and this leads us to Bobito Garcia, the DJ basketball player…he does everything. He's like a sneaker pimp. So, he invited us over to his house, and we went over there, and he opened up his closet, and there was this wall just full of sneakers! He pulled out one after another, and he knew everything—like what the sole was made out of, what kind of stitching, what kind of leather, where it was from originally, and where it was manufactured. I mean, he probably knew more shit than some of the sneaker designers. So, then Nike started calling and were like, "Yo, who is this guy? We want him." They put him under contract.

RM: To do what?

YK: To just advise them. To consult about basketball, because he knew everything inside out. He played pro in Puerto Rico and semi-pro here.

That was the beginning of when I started seeing corporations tapping into the kids. And then my next project was the NYC Yoke campaign. That's when we started going out and talking to people in the streets and getting responses. When we had a new line of shoes come out and we wanted to get feedback, instead of doing a focus group, we just went out on the street asking the kids, "Yo, what do you think of these shoes?" Nike started using Shadi and Bobito and all these other people. I kept telling Nike that they have to keep in touch with these guys, and that they have to have a relationship with them. But Nike just blew them off once they were done with them and moved on.

RM: And what was their reaction to that?

YK: I think from that these kids learned. And this was 10, 15 years ago. That was the beginning of the corporations going out into the streets and getting these street-savvy kids to work for them. I've always kept in touch with everyone. But Nike doesn't know how to communicate. All they know is how to use these kids and then they're done. So, I was on that other side. I was on Nike's side, but I kept telling them, "You can't do this."

RM: Right. It's going to backfire.

YK: Right, and now it's the same thing. So many kids are so savvy. They know what these corporations are doing. You've got And One, Nike, Adidas, etc. going out to Rutgers Summer Tournaments scoping out what's going on. You can spot these guys from miles. You can tell they're the sneaker people. So instead of saying "Fuck you, we're not going to sell out," the kids are saying, well, you know what, we're going to make some money, too.

RM: And do you think they're doing it honestly

with the intent of genuinely helping out these companies? Or are they doing it in a way to subvert them and get paid to lie?

YK: I don't know what they're thinking. I always tell everyone to fucking get whatever they can get out of these people, because that's what they're doing to you. They don't care. They're not doing this to promote you. They're doing it for themselves. So, you have to cash in as much as you can, because they're going to drop you when they're done. I think this new generation has toughened up and gotten a lot smarter about this. They realize that the corporations are going to make money off them, so they might as well make money off the corporations. Ten years ago we were just, "Yeah, send him my sneakers." We had these graffiti guys doing stuff for us, and we just sent them the sneakers. Not anymore.

RM: Are you familiar with the Presto ad campaign where they wouldn't allow the artists' signatures on their own artwork?

YK: Yeah. This thing's not going to last too long with Nike. They just bulldoze into the street art scene. I know about the Alife show in LA. Alife created this whole concept store, and Nike pretty much bulldozed into that LA show. They started telling them, "You can't have that, and you can't have this, and you can only have that." They didn't want the competitor's shoes in there or anything. I mean, it wasn't Nike's show.

RM: Well, they could argue that it was their show if they're paying the bill.

YK: But it wasn't presented that way. It wasn't like, "Nike is offering you to come and have a show." It was the gallery's call. They invited Alife to come and have this show, and then said, "Oh,

by the way, Nike's sponsoring this, so we need to follow their rules." I've been with Nike, and they are the fucking most evil one out of them all.

RM: Tell me about this Suit Man exhibition.

YK: I got two thousand dollars for putting those logos on my poster. I think Adidas paid for an ad, and then Tokion magazine printed the invitation.

RM: Was this Suit Man concept something that you approached Adidas about?

YK: No. I got a call one day: "Yo man, Adidas wants to sponsor you." I said, "Yeah, what does that mean?" "They will give you some money and they will take care of the booze and invitation and do something like a little mailer or something." I already had the show lined up. They didn't influence me with the work. All they wanted to do was put their logo in there.

RM: Was there anything objectionable in the work that they had a problem with?

YK: No. Actually they were really cool, because that work is from twelve years of my life—six of which I was traveling through Nike jobs. I had Little Penny in there and Charles Barkley, Carl Louis, and all these Nike athletes in there. But I told them from the beginning, "I'm not going to edit this stuff out just because you're Adidas," and they were cool about it.

RM: Do you feel their sponsorship was more on the patron level?

YK: Yeah, definitely more on that level.

RM: They wanted their logo on the exhibition poster. Did they want it anywhere else?

YK: No. Actually, I had it bigger on the poster, and they said, "No, we don't need it really big. Just make it smaller." Abby from Adidas knows what's going on in the street. She keeps in touch with artists. She keeps in touch with everybody. I don't know anyone like that at Nike who does that kind of thing. She's full-time for Adidas, and she knows to keep in touch with everybody.

RM: Have you been able to film Suit Man on a shoot and then use that for your own work?

YK: I have to get something out of it. That Nike global Olympic campaign took me around the whole world. I just put myself in it as a cameo in each location. You know, I was working for this major corporation. I was really naïve, and I was a lot younger, too. I worked for one of the best companies, and I gave them everything I had. I worked fucking eighteen, twenty hours a day for this company. I treated it like my company. I had so much passion. They were always telling me, "Yeah, you're the key player of this company. We can't do anything without you." I believed that whole spiel—being part of the team and all that. Then I slowly realized, as I got wiser, I'm just a cog in their machine. No matter how hard I work, it's still not a part of me. It's not a piece of my thing. So I was feeling kind of lost in direction, like, where do I go? I'm an advertising guy, not from the heart, but somehow I just fell into this whole thing. So, I decided I'm going to get something out of this. Every shoot I go to, I wear my suit. Every photo shoot and TV shoot I do, I wear my work suit, and I wear my glasses. Somehow I get myself in there, and then slowly put myself in a spot. When everything's shot, I go in a separate editing room with another editor and cut my own version of the commercial with me in it. It's like a signature. I slowly developed this reel where I'm in a Nike spot, ESPN commercial, etc. That's how Suit Man got to the next level.

RM: So you've got this body of work thanks to your position. Thanks to your clients.

YK: Yeah, thanks to the corporate world of America, I guess. But that doesn't count as sponsorship. They don't know I'm doing this.

RM: Let me ask you specifically about the Adidas involvement with Suit Man. Is the exhibition being taken to Tokyo?

YK: They approached me about incorporating one of their characters into my exhibition in order to create a more sales-driven show for Adidas products—the kind of show where you can hang up pictures next to the clothes. I don't want my work to be showcased like that. So, I proposed that we keep all the shopping on the second floor and clear-out all of the first floor, and that would be the exhibition. I wanted to solve this problem. I didn't want to just walk away and just say no. That's where my advertising background comes in. I still want to solve this problem. I still want to bring the sales in.

RM: Is this to say that you believe in Adidas, and you want to support them? You want to assume their problems and solve them?

YK: There are two things I believe in: one is that I really want to get my work out there for people to see. And the second thing is that I want to solve the problem for Adidas, because there are things that I want to do in the future, and maybe they can help me.

RM: Why do you feel inclined to make it work?

YK: It's hard. At the end of the day, I've got to fucking pay my bills. I've got to live, and I just can't do that with my work. Only a few people appreciate it. When people ask me, "How much is that print?" I don't know the price. I don't know, because it's so personal for me. If I'm going to let it go, it has to be to someone that I know—someone who appreciates it. I don't want to give it to some stranger.

RM: Do think your hesitation about commodifying your own work holds you back so that you have to rely on the advertising world?

YK: I think you're right. Absolutely right. It has been holding me back. I hadn't been showing my work to too many people until that Alife show. It's like something that I did on my own. I'm really grateful to Rob and those guys, because I came out of left field. They've always been showing graffiti stuff. Most people were like, "Who is this fucking guy?" A lot of people didn't know who I was.

RM: Moving forward with your work, do you see a clear separation between the commercials and the artwork? Or are the two merging more?

YK: Merging more. That's where it's at. A commercial is a very powerful medium. It gets out there to millions of people.

RM: Has there been a time or situation where companies want Suit Man?

YK: I once got a call from Amstel Light beer. By the way, beware of young, hip, cool, advertising agency creatives. They usually wear a wallet with a big chain, have a goatee, wear big baggy Diesel pants. I think they hang out at a lot of cool bars, and they have a shitload of money and buy a lot of drinks. Beware of those kinds of people, because I met this one guy... I was sharing my Suit Man idea with him, and he was, "Oh that's great. I want to get your number." He calls me up a couple of weeks later, "Can you send me

everything you have on Suit Man? I'm pitching for Amstel Light. You'll be a great spokesman." So, I sent him my Suit Man reel, and I don't hear from him. Amstel Light didn't buy it. And then about a year later, I get like three phone calls on my machine like, "Hey is that you on the commercial?" "Yeah, this commercial has you in it. It's this Asian guy with glasses and a suit just sitting there. He doesn't do anything." There's a close-up of his head and the tie, and even my sister calls me up and is like, "Oh my God. I saw you on TV and blah blah blah." I got so many calls and I thought, whoa man, this is fucking weird. So I tracked it down and found out it was one of the creative guys who pitched it for Amstel. He re-pitched it to another client—some dot com company, and then he didn't call me. He just got some other Asian guy in a suit and glasses just sitting in a chair, and he doesn't move, and the camera moves around...all the same as Suit Man.

RM: That's just it. People in that world just take. Take. Take. Take. Take. How was that resolved?

YK: It wasn't. See, that's the thing. In the advertising world, anything goes. Talk is cheap. You can have great fucking ideas, you can talk to your friends about it, but if you don't act on it...

RM: Where do you think all of this sponsorship is going?

YK: In general, I think it's going to get ugly. The people who are getting down with corporations are going to realize that these companies are not paying as much money as they should. These sponsorship projects with artists are cutting out advertising. These artists haven't been making jack shit compared to what an advertising agency charges. When you pick up *Ad Week* and read in the beginning who is pitching for what—you see, it's like five million dollar accounts, twenty million dollar accounts, two million dollar accounts. That's what artists should be getting, because they're creating the same results for these companies. These corporations are teaming up with these artists to do things and are going, "We got a fucking deal now!" They get these fucking artists and just drop them a hundred thousand dollars, and get the same amount of impact that these fucking agencies get for them.

RM: A lot of these corporations try to play the "exposure" card.

YK: That's the thing. They don't know what's going on. They don't know how these artists feel. They still think that you're getting "exposure." They don't know what's really going on. People are like, "We've had enough with fucking Nike and Adidas and Altoids or whomever. We don't even want that kind of exposure."

RM: Does corporate sponsorship push art more towards the entertainment industry?

YK: I think it does; that's just where the culture is going. I think artists want to be treated like celebrities.

RM: Being a celebrity means being in the service industry, which is what the entertainment industry is. They figure out what the people want, or try to guess what they will want, test it, market it, and produce the deliverables. Will artists become simply tools to facilitate that process like celebrities? I mean, the same thing has been happening to the sports industry for years.

YK: That's true. I think the majority of artists will turn it around. The difference between the athletes and the artists is that there's a lot more camaraderie in artist groups. There's a little bit more loyalty on the street level—a little more respect. That could be the only hope for this scene to break out from the corporate world and still get on top.

RM: How do you end up on top?

YK: Take advantage of the corporate offers. I think our circle is pretty tight—you and Alife and with everybody in that scene—we all kind of respect each other. We don't step on each others' feet. One person can stand up and say something when a corporation tries to come in. That's the only way that we can fight the corporate take-over of this art scene.

RM: Have you thought of other ways of funding your Suit Man project?

YK: Doing these shoots is a lot easier for me than writing grants, and one way or another, I have to kiss someone's ass. This way, I really have a connection—I have a job. I get to fly down to South Africa to shoot a helicopter scene and then stop everything to go stand in the middle of the production to be filmed. You can get grants, but I don't know if you can get a million-dollar grant. People tell me you can get grants ten or twenty grand, max. Maybe a hundred grand. What can you do with that? I mean, I could do something with it, but not a big production where I have snowmobiles up in a snow slope with Evel Knievel sitting next to me. I'd need a few hundred thousand dollars or a million dollars. This is an easier way for me to do that.

"That's the problem with corporate collaborations. If you say no, there are 100,000 desperate 'designers' waiting in line ready to copy your work. You can never win."

BARRY McGEE (TWIST)

Barry McGee

Barry McGee (TWIST) is an artist who lives and works in San Francisco and has exhibited his work internationally. He recently participated in the Liverpool Biennial.

RM: What corporate-sponsored projects have you been involved in?

BM: I guess the most recent was a billboard project in Los Angeles, curated by Aaron Rose and backed by Nike. It was pretty much a free-for-all, except for a Nike swoosh on the wood structure of the billboard.

RM: The Nike swoosh doesn't seem too invasive; however, it still exists and even serves as a signature of sorts to let the world know who has authored (or at least backed) the piece. Did you ever see this as a problem?

BM: Sure, it was invasive. I believe Aaron Rose broke off the swoosh with a hammer—a move I applauded. But later we were told, "it must be in place." Somewhere down the line, I'm sure I will regret doing this project, but for now it was a message that was pro-graffiti in a town with a mayor who lists graffiti as his number one enemy. If it makes even one person angry, I am a happy man. What really gets me is these kids in their Hondas who have their friends cutting vinyl swooshes for the back windows of their cars. I've heard Nike has been cracking down and trying to prosecute them and confiscating the plotters as evidence of copyright infringement. Maybe that would have been a better billboard.

RM: Can you provide any insight into the Tokion figurine project you did? That seems like it was a good match between an artist and a company?

BM: That was fun.

RM: What are your thoughts on that Calvin Klein project?

BM: Those stupid "limited-edition" fragrance bottles? They asked me if I would like to present a design for them, and I whole-heartedly said no.

Those things are worse than that guy faking "Barry McGee" bottles online. That's the problem with corporate collaborations. If you say no, there are 100,000 desperate "designers" waiting in line ready to copy your work. You can never win.

RM: What are the motives for artists and corporations to work together?

BM: That pesky thing called money. The corporation gets the instant credibility of an artist's endorsement, which will make them millions of dollars in the long run, and the artist gets somewhere between six to eight thousand dollars and a pair of dumb shoes that will last them a few months.

RM: Would you work with Nike again?

BM: I would like to work with Nike to further that "accident" where Nike shoes were lost at sea, and then washed up on shorelines. Perhaps they can drop an equal amount of right shoes in the ocean to follow up on that campaign. I wear Clarks, so if they ever wanted to work out a sponsorship deal, I might be interested.

RM: How was the recent *Scribble & Scripture* exhibition in regards to corporate sponsorship?

BM: It was fine, I guess. In the eighties there were art foundations with their logos at the bottom of announcement cards. Every once in a while there would be a Wal-Mart or Target sponsorship. Then in the '90s, Phillip-Morris was in the fine print. Now in 2003, I find Nike swooshes and Vitamin Water (whatever the hell that is). I'm sure this discussion will continue for some time.

"I think a lot of companies are trying techniques like 'artist-designed' exclusive pieces or introducing a new product in a gallery-like situation in order to create a buzz with trend-setters, but more specifically, to attract jaded consumers."

Bill McMullen

Bill McMullen

Bill McMullen is the former Senior Art Director at Def Jam Records and currently is a graphic designer and video director in New York. His clients include The Beastie Boys, Criterion, Atlantic Records, and MTV. Bill also co-owns the clothing label, SwishNYC. (swishnyc.com)

RM: What corporate-sponsored projects have you been involved in?

BM: Well, indirectly, most of what I do is corporate sponsored. I am primarily involved in the graphic arts, so I fall under the category of corporate more often than fine arts. I am often asked to create to sell rather than create for the sake of creation.

RM: This difference between graphic and fine arts is at the heart of many of these artist/company relationships. How do you further define the difference between graphic and fine art?

BM: To me, graphic arts are used to communicate a purpose or agenda within the structure of mass reproduction and cost-effectiveness, in a timely manner. It feels like many fine artists are more concerned with communicating emotion than "This event is on Sunday at 8pm."

I think with graphic arts, the foremost goal is communication of an idea. But fine arts can also communicate an idea. So where is the line? I put the line at reproduction, where fine art tends to be a singular work or piece, versus 10,000 4-over-1 flyers. I think graphic arts have really moved into prominence in the last 40 to 50 years. Even fine art movements in the 1950s and 1960s, op and pop art movements, for example, were using flat fields of color, shapes and even motives seen primarily in advertising. I'll cite Andy Warhol's Campbell's soup cans—a concept being moved from everyday life, and placed in the setting of art—and utilizing techniques not that far off from what Campbell's does when they make labels for their actual cans. Warhol used silkscreening, a technique developed for mass reproduction and consistency regardless of the operator actually making the print. Anyway, a company can relate to the mass-production and cost-effectiveness of art created this way and can fold it into it's advertising. A set amount of resources are set aside by a company for advertising, and a dynamic, effective gimmick can make the most of that investment. So I think a lot of companies are trying techniques like "artist-designed" exclusive pieces or introducing a new product in a gallery-like situation in order to create a buzz with trend-setters, but more specifically, to attract jaded consumers.

RM: So, then, what "designer-designed" works have you created with a company?

BM: Well, a few years ago, I did a co-branded t-shirt with Sony, Japan, and my company, SwishNYC.

RM: Ok, right there, I think this raises another issue that seems to be unique to our generation of artists: Creating work under pseudonyms or even creating companies and making work under a company name. In your case, SwishNYC is your company, which serves as an outlet for your work. Do you create work under your birth name? The reason for using graffiti names is obvious, but why a company name, and furthermore, why do you think artists are creating their own companies?

BM: Well, I am moving toward that in my own work, but I think right now people need something to latch onto, as in, "He's the guy who did blank" or "That's the company that did blank" before they sit down and fully accept it. I think people filter out what or who they don't know about yet if it feels like too much. There is so much work being done right now, great work at that, and it feels like overload. So in this project, the popularity of my work under our company name created the need to include us, not necessarily my work under my birth name. Quite simply, people probably don't know who I am, but this market knew who SwishNYC was. And a company name can be used for work rather than art.

RM: Back to your example…

BM: We did a design on the front, and the back says, "It's Time To ROCK STAR." Sony, Japan, was confused. They didn't immediately understand the play on the weird little shirts you see over there with crazy English phrases (see engrish.com). It took a few discussions, and after they were convinced we weren't making fun of them, they finally agreed to let it go through. Which is why I bring this whole thing up. What I had done was questioned, and I had to justify it to allow it to be used. I can understand. It was a paying project, not my own art or statement, and they needed something that would represent them and sell. So I wound up under what I call their umbrella. However, in an art show underwritten by a company, this umbrella may not be so apparent to the artist involved. What if the artist creates something the underwriter can't use, doesn't want, or doesn't want the public to think about? Questions can be raised about the purpose and intent of the show, as well as the benefits or disadvantages.

RM: Exactly. A lot of times the real agenda is masked with these sponsored art shows and projects. If the agendas match, then it's a good fit for both parties. What are the pros and cons for artists working with corporations?

BM: On the upside for the artist, a project that might be cost-prohibitive for an individual could be funded by a corporation. Or, locale or audience formerly unobtainable by the artist may be reached. Exposure can be high and can springboard the artist to other projects. On the downside, should the artist create something that misrepresents or offends the company, the funding may cease or, at best, continue with stipulations for the artist, or guidelines of behavior, so to speak. Also at stake can be the credibility of the artist—loss of core audience, stigma of "sell-out," or ironically, loss of opportunities to work with other companies. For the company, the benefits can be "street cred" and approval from a tough audience—cynical and fickle influential-types that could spark a beneficial trend in purchasing or public opinion. Image can be improved or maintained by aligning with influential artists, or, should I say, "influential, recognizable, popular artists presenting only brand-positive concepts and images." It seems many artists participating in corporate-sponsored shows tune-out the relationship with the company or subconsciously follow guidelines that are implied by entering the relationship. The rationale may be that the exposure, experience, and opportunity outweigh the risks of the downside.

RM: For example?

BM: An example would be the many "shows" we have seen where street-level (re: graf) or underground artists are asked to take a vanilla version of a product and paint or stylize it as they wish. Puma just did one with soccer balls. The Adidas Shelltoe shows come to mind, as curators invite graffiti artists to take a shelltoe sneaker and flip it in their style. Fresh, notable artists are picked and the company benefits from alignment with what is happening in the underground. In this instance, the art is created after the concept of the show and becomes secondary. Consciously or not, all of the artists in these shows have made decisions to avoid insulting Adidas, and therefore, Adidas has influenced the art. An example of what might not make it into one of these shows: an Adidas Shelltoe sneaker I have spray-painted to look like a Nike sneaker. Not really congruent with the underlying message of the "art" show. The chances are high the shoe would be withheld. This is a simplistic and obvious example to make a point: being invited to be in such a show and participating means that artists involved have agreed to play ball by operating within certain safe boundaries that keep the company in a positive light.

RM: The same can be said of the art market in general. Trends and aesthetics come and go, and there's a huge group of strictly gallery artists who go with the flow and create collector-acceptable work instead of defining those trends and showing people new ways of looking at the world. There's a support system for those kinds of artists where the creation of perceived value is used in the design of the display of the work with stark and sterile gallery environments.

BM: Many of those interested in the paradox of your *Sponsorship* show are probably familiar with the book *No Logo*. The author, Naomi Klein, discusses a series of live music shows sponsored by a beer company in which moderately famous bands would play at a "Miller Beer Night," in small venues the band could probably fill four or five times over. The idea being you got to see a "cool" band in a close space and you had such a great time that now you can't seem to differentiate

fun from Miller Beer. After several shows, market research divulged that few people cared about anything but the band, and even fewer remembered the sponsoring company. So the tactic was switched: the name-brand bands were still hired, but now it became a "secret" show, a free grab-bag put on by Miller Beer, thus switching emphasis back to the company. The point? Corporate sponsorship is a form of advertising, and the company probably expects recognition.

RM: Of course we don't want to over-generalize, because some of these companies are more philanthropic than others.

BM: Yeah, I agree. It's not always evil. Artists are people, and people need to eat, and most want to improve their living situation. And not every piece of art needs to fuck with the system. But many companies, although sincere in their efforts, still spread their umbrella over the project. The company cannot really be faulted. By definition they are in it to make that dolo, kid—ultimately, the artist needs to decide if financial backing and exposure are worth more than absolute creative control.

RM: We're back to the classic question: How do artists fund their production and careers? One of the things I'm trying to define with this exhibition and book is a new patronage system that ignores government art grants, individual patrons, and even the traditional gallery system. What other options do you see for artists?

BM: That's a tough question. If I could answer that, I would probably be making a lot more money. I think many artists are creating these objects, toys, or t-shirts to generate money and awareness. Options for artists? Well, I would love to say the traditional gallery system could be moved to the internet, with virtual-goggle openings and faxable refreshments, but I think people enjoy seeing the craft in person, at set times. Seeing other people that they can have open dialogs with about the art. I really like seeing a well-painted piece or a well-crafted object, and I don't think photos, blogs, or web pages can always properly convey this. I also see this huge wave of beautifully designed and well-printed books, showcasing the artists' work in an affordable collection. You may not be able to afford the painting itself, but you can probably buy the book or DVD. There are small publishers working hard to bring cool, collectible books to the market, and in turn, small cool outlets that can sell these books. And small gallery-like shows within these outlets to punctuate the release of the book. Here artists should be careful to avoid getting the very short end of the stick if the product is moving because of his or her popularity. I think these times are forcing artists to treat themselves like a product or situation that may require management or creative representation, and ultimately legal protection. Or you can just say fuck it, and rock some graf burners; some may find that easier than all this nonsense. I think the artists need to take a serious look at what they want to accomplish in their work, and how far they want to go in terms of living off of their art.

Christian Strike

Christian Strike was the founder and president of Strength Magazine *from 1995 to 2002. He is a co-founder of Iconoclast Productions, a project-based company working in collaboration with artists and institutions to produce a wide variety of multi-media endeavors.*

RM: What corporate-sponsored projects have you been involved in?

CS: A lot. I don't know where to begin. The biggest one, over the longest period of time, was the magazine I founded and later sold to a publicly owned media and marketing services company. It's called *Strength*, and it's a skateboard magazine with a particular focus on the art of skateboard culture. While I ran the magazine, we did numerous projects with corporations outside of basic print advertising, which typically defines a magazine's relationship with other corporate entities. Not that it's art related but…

RM: I actually think it is art-related. That magazine was your art, and your role as an artist was more curatorial. But anyway…

CS: In conjunction with Converse, we produced an amateur skate contest held at Skater's Island in Providence, Rhode Island in 1999. Also in 1999, I licensed the magazine's name to London/Mo Wax/ffrr Records (a division of Time Warner) for a music compilation that I executive produced. It was called *Strength Magazine presents Subtext.* Barry McGee and Phil Frost collaborated on the album cover art work. That year, the magazine and London Records also sponsored a show at Alleged in New York called *Coup d'Etat*, curated by Phil Frost and Aaron Rose.

RM: So with the magazine, you were in the unique position of being sponsored, and you also sponsored projects. When you sponsored that show, what exactly was the magazine's role?

CS: We, along with London Records, basically provided financial support for the show. The sponsorship helped fund the promotional efforts for the show: printing flyers, advertising for the show, etc. The Alleged show happened at about the same time as the *Subtext* album release, so given Phil's involvement in both projects, the sponsorship of *Coup d'Etat* made sense.

RM: Did *Strength* sponsor anything else?

CS: An ongoing project we did through the magazine was also working with individual artists to design limited-edition covers, be featured in articles, and produce assorted limited products (t-shirts, skateboards, etc.) to commemorate the release of that particular issue. We basically started that whole thing back in the mid '90s, which now seems to have become a very popular trend among magazines, clothing and shoe brands. Maybe we didn't "start" the whole thing, but certainly at the time, nobody was doing what we were doing…all of which now seems very commonplace.

RM: You can say you started that trend, for the record. I'll support that. There seems to be a lot of fine art and commercial art crossover, to the point where distinguishing the two seems moot.

CS: I mean, Warhol got his start while working as a commercial artist drawing women's shoes. Commercial work seems to be an established avenue for artists, and this is not new. However, I think that relationship between commercial work versus art for the artist's sake is far more prevalent in the circle of artists I work with. And it's not always "commercial" work I am referencing either. Most of it is DIY, self-produced, self-published work that may take form as zines, record covers, self-published books, whatever. In my opinion, this is what makes art important. Artists who have developed a "fan base" if you will, not through manufactured means of exclusive galleries, haughty museums and perceived

"Artists who have developed a 'fan base' through grass-roots level activities and conduits…those are the ones whose work resonates most in our culture and, therefore, are the most relevant and important."

CHRISTIAN STRIKE

value, but through grass-roots level activities and conduits…those are the ones whose work resonates most in our culture and, therefore, are the most relevant and important.

RM: Yes, this trend of artist no longer needing to rely on old systems of production and distribution is something that seems to define this group. However, instead of self-publishing, in many instances artists are working with companies to make these more accessible items. Can you comment on not the DIY element per se, but the fact that companies and artists are working together to created limited-edition widgets.

CS: It totally makes sense. The artist stands to gain by having an entity subsidize making their art accessible so that everyone can buy it, thus broadening the audience for their work. The company stands to gain by aligning their brand with an artist who may be perceived as being hip or having street credibility.

RM: I remember when you asked me to do some shirts and a cover for *Strength*. I was down to do it, because (at that time, I believe) the magazine was independent, it supported and believed in cool artists, and it was an opportunity to share my work with the people whom I believe, would most appreciate it. There seemed to be a mutual support, or at least a mutual and equal exploitation. In working with any of these artists, did you ever feel the relationship wasn't mutually beneficial and equal?

CS: Not really. I think both parties benefited from the projects equally. They always took several months to coordinate and execute, so if sometime during the process it became obvious one party wasn't getting the value they deserved,

I addressed and corrected it before the project wrapped,…or at least I think I did!

RM: So, potential problems were averted because, in your role as head of the company, you were hands-on. This is actually something I look for in the companies I work with. Will I be working with the head of the company or passed off to an underling? Artists are the heads of their own companies, so it's only fair that the two parties communicate on that equal level.

CS: I agree for the most part. I'm sure there may be instances, perhaps from a technical or manufacturing aspect, where it makes sense for the artist to work directly with someone who is involved heavily in those areas, beyond the company owner. For instance, with DC Shoes' *Artist Projects*, I'm sure those artists end up working with production staff other than Damon Way, who is the owner and leader of those projects. In that instance I think it's totally appropriate, and it'd be hard to criticize a situation like that, since there probably isn't anyone who has supported artists more than someone like Damon. Believe me, those projects are done completely out of his pure interest to help and support artists who come from skateboard culture.

RM: Absolutely. DC is certainly a special case. OK, so now what are you working on?

CS: More recently, through our project-based company, Iconoclast, Aaron Rose and I are curating a group exhibition to debut in Spring 2004 at the CAC (contemporaryartscenter.org) in Cincinnati, in their new building designed by Zaha Hadid. The exhibit will then tour to other major contemporary art museums (such as the Yerba Buena in San Francisco) both nationally as well as abroad. The exhibition's tour will be sponsored by at least one major corporation that I cannot yet name. To revolve around that, we will also produce ancillary products with the featured artists, and those may or may not involve partnerships with corporate sponsors.

RM: As you move ahead with the traveling museum show, what will you look for in the various sponsorship relationships?

CS: It will basically be the same thing you see with other major museum shows, in that a corporate sponsor typically underwrites the show, and in return, is the presenter for the exhibition. For instance, Merrill Lynch sponsored the Warhol retrospective at the MOCA in LA. Merrill Lynch's name is listed as the presenter of the exhibit and appears on all collateral, advertising, and in the catalog.

RM: Is there a debate surrounding just how loud that company's presence will be?

CS: Not really. Nor do I think there will be since, again, it won't be any different than what typically goes on at museum exhibitions.

RM: And you're curating smaller shows?

CS: In February 2003, Aaron curated *Scribble & Scripture*, a Barry McGee, Phil Frost and Thomas Campbell show at the Roberts & Tilton gallery in LA. In addition to the original art available, Iconoclast produced an edition of screen prints with each artist. These will be sold at Roberts & Tilton in LA, as well as in other galleries and boutiques. They are really special, as each artist painted or drew on each print, in effect making each print an original.

RM: With this exhibition, you could say that the gallery is sponsoring the show, to a degree, in that they are hosting the exhibition and perhaps even fronting the money for the prints. What are the details of that relationship? How do you feel about logos appearing on the bottom of prints?

CS: For this show, Nike was actually the sponsor. Their name appeared on the collateral, advertising, etc. The screen print editions do not feature any logos. The prints are purely art, and we did not want to interfere with that in any way.

RM: I want to address the idea of "pure art," as you mentioned. It seems that these prints are held in high regard, and therefore shouldn't be soiled with a logo. What exactly is "pure art?"

CS: Well, I think there would certainly be a difference if the prints had any kind of logo on them. The paintings in the show didn't have a logo on them, so neither should the prints. At least that was our perspective. The truth of the matter is, the issue never even entered our minds.

RM: And your Nike project?

CS: Aaron worked on a project with Nike where three artists were commissioned to create a mural to last for 3 months each on a billboard on the corner of La Brea and Beverly, right above the Stüssy and Undefeated stores. He worked with Barry, Geoff McFetridge and Dennis Hopper on that one.

RM: What are the exact details of this? Is the Nike swoosh on the billboards? What's in it for the artists and for Nike?

CS: The Swoosh only appears on the base of the billboard. The idea is basically that a more subtle, honest approach to marketing is really what works. For instance, to most people, a Barry McGee mural on a billboard looks like common graffiti. The people who know, know. Meaning, those who are familiar with Barry's work will also know Nike sponsored it. You don't need a gigantic Swoosh slapping you in the face to get the message across. But Nike's goal really wasn't to necessarily do this as some huge advertising campaign. It's just their desire to support something artistic and cultural that deserves to be supported.

RM: And for the people who don't know Barry's work but do know Nike, do you think Barry, to them, now becomes "that Nike artist?" This is unlikely, I know, but you know what I'm saying.

CS: I seriously doubt it. Again, since the swoosh is barely there, most people, in this instance, will not even know that it's Nike's billboard. Again, those who know, know. And that was Nike's goal. Now, if Nike sponsored and paid some artist to launch a massive print and TV advertising campaign, then sure, that artist would probably become known to some degree as "that Nike artist."

RM: Also, do you think Nike would have agreed to not put their swoosh on at all? Do you foresee a day when a corporation's motives could be so purely altruistic?

CS: I think we could all probably guess and debate about that until the cows come home. However, I think Nike could have possibly achieved its goal without their logo. There was print collateral and an opening party at the site of the billboard, and I think that would have had a similar impact.

RM: What are the integrity issues that need to be addressed with such projects?

CS: When I did the magazine, there weren't that many issues of integrity to worry about, to be really frank. I mean, a magazine is a content and marketing vehicle. Once you cross the line from a really personal, not-for-profit "zine" made for you and your friends, to a magazine sold on newsstands (which is what happened in my case), your publication is a marketing vehicle, plain and simple. Our goal at that point was to just try to offer the readers something they couldn't find elsewhere, content wise. Otherwise, we weren't doing them a service, nor our advertisers.

RM: I like that you make this distinction and are very clear about a commercial magazine's role in culture. So, to move beyond that, were there any ads that you would not accept, because you did not believe they should be in your magazine? Did you run tobacco or alcohol ads in *Strength* knowing that your readers were young and impressionable?

CS: No, of course not. Tobacco and alcohol ads were off limits.

RM: And with Iconoclast?

CS: With Iconoclast, we are very selective in what we do. For instance, the project has to come from our ideas, and it has to be forcing issues in some kind of way. The museum show is something we had already packaged when the museum approached us. Same thing with marketing projects for companies such as Nike. There isn't even any Nike rhetoric on those billboards. You don't need to beat people over the head to get the message across. That's what we're about, presenting things in new, more effective ways.

RM: How did the artists feel about being supported by Nike and, in turn, supporting Nike with their work? Was there a dialogue between the artists and the company about what exactly this project meant and what the goals were?

■

■

CS: To be honest, I'm not sure. You'd have to ask them for that answer.

RM: What are the motives for artists and corporations to work together?

CS: Obviously the goal of a brand and/or corporation is to sell more of its products. Historically, "art" has never been a great seller of products to the mainstream. I mean, getting a current art star like Damian Hirst to hawk Pepsi is not going to have the effect on their sales that Britney Spears did.

RM: And what if Damien Hirst were a spokesperson for Pepsi (or any other major brand)? Would your perception of him or his work change? Or for any artist?

CS: I don't know. It may not, given my current perception of Damien Hirst. However, there are certainly other artists for whom, if they became a spokesperson for Pepsi, my perception would probably change.

RM: So, perhaps there is this issue or perception of "sell-out" that finds its way into the visual arts? Have you ever changed your opinion of an artist based on his or her deciding to work with a certain corporation?

CS: The issue of "sell-out" exists just about everywhere with everything. I can't think of a situation where my opinion has changed in that regard.

RM: Do you remember all those ads Andy Warhol did for cameras, hair products, etc.? Do you think he paved the way for celebrity artists to be spokespersons with integrity? I can't think of any other visual fine artist spokespersons, can you?

CS: Warhol was clearly an aberration, in that he was on such a different level than just about everyone else. But yes, I do think he paved the

way for a lot of things.

RM: So what is art's role in these corporate marketing plans?

CS: Art does have a big effect but in a much more indirect way. However, these corporations are starting to get clever and are realizing that the same advertising/corporate message will not resonate with everyone. So they're subdividing, specializing, and focusing their marketing efforts to target smaller, more niche groups like skaters, music heads, whomever.

RM: So is art's role in these strategies simply to appeal to these niche groups? Is this art as decoration, or does art play a more important role? And if so, then aren't these corporations just preaching to the converted? Wouldn't it be riskier, more daring, and more important if the companies tried to bring the work to a new audience?

CS: Yes, clearly the art's role in those cases is to appeal to niche groups. I don't think it's about preaching to the converted. Again, I feel that the company's goal is to align their brand with the image of the artist, therefore improving their brand's image. In effect, preaching the company's brand to the "converted," as you call them, with the art or artist as the conduit.

RM: This niche marketing strategy seems to parallel the fragmented art market as well. This subculture of artists we're talking about certainly isn't selling their work to the same collectors as some of the larger galleries and certainly not at the same prices. And actually, it seems like their audience is larger. These artists are reaching a broader audience.

CS: That's the thing I was saying earlier. In that circle of artists I am familiar with, the audience is huge, which in my opinion makes them so much more relevant than those who don't have that same kind of base support. They built their audiences through honest hard work and grass-roots level projects, not through hype, personal agendas and other manufactured means so prevalent in the established art world. How do you value art? You're going to tell me that some Julian Schnabel painting is worth more than a Phil Frost or Ed Templeton painting? On one hand, you have some guy who really only ever appealed, and only for a short time, to a very small audience of stuffy gallery owners, rich patrons, celebrities and museum folk. On the other hand, with Phil or Ed, you have someone whose work and career is closely followed by tens of thousands of people. And I'm not even exaggerating. In fact, I'm probably being very, very conservative with those numbers. Did you see the turnout at the opening of your group skate show at Deitch? Are you going to tell me Schnabel or Kenny Scharf had an opening like that? Maybe they did, but I don't think so.

RM: This is a question that has come up in some of the other interviews, and I want to get your opinion on it based on your last comment. If we're judging artists based on popularity, then do we throw out the quality of these audiences? I mean, sure, thousands attend these shows, but who is buying the work? Can this fan base financially support this group? Furthermore, by extending this logic of numbers, why aren't we championing the WWF as the next big art movement? Do you see a difference between quantity and quality of audience? I know it seems crappy to put people in those terms, but those are the terms that the exclusionary art world uses.

CS: Clearly it's not only about popularity. And to me, it's not about the quality of the audience either; it's the quality of the art. In the instances and artists I'm referring to, the quality of the art is phenomenal, which is why it resonates with so many people. People like Phil Frost and Barry McGee hold their own.

RM: Do you think we're hitting upon an art vs. entertainment issue here? Certainly there is more support for "artists" who work in the corporate-supported entertainment industry (the recording industry, for instance). Do you see any kind of parallel system that could work for visual artists?

CS: Not one that I can really think of.

"Times are definitely changing, and art is changing. That's why it's a little hard to know exactly what's going on and how to treat it, because it's all so new."

ROMON YANG (RO-STARR)

Romon Yang

Romon Yang (RO-STARR) is an artist who lives and works in Brooklyn, New York. He describes making art as a "creative journey of discovery that each artist must seek inside themselves. I am constantly challenging myself to change and inspire."

RM: What different sponsorship projects have you taken on?

RO-STARR: Well, I've done projects with Gravis, Agnés B., Yamaha, Nike, Levi's, Adidas…

RM: What was the whole Gravis project about?

RO-STARR: I met some of the Gravis people at the *Winter Music Conference* in 2001. It's a long drawn-out story. I guess they wanted to do something different with Gravis, so they sponsored a live painting event with the Ink Heads, Barnstormers, and Heavy Weights in 2002. From that, they felt that sponsoring an artist was a good thing. They felt it was a very marketable thing, so they sponsored me in the same way a pro surfer or snow boarder would be sponsored.

RM: So, what does it mean to be sponsored by Gravis?

RO-STARR: The deal was a 1-year contract that basically entailed doing two advertisements. I got a salary as a team member and got to do some special products as well. Actually, the products were separate from the contract.

RM: A salary in exchange for appearing in ads and creating artwork for them?

RO-STARR: Well, on one advertisement, I painted on a canvas output that had a shoe on it.

RM: They sent you a canvas with a picture of a shoe on it?

RO-STARR: Yeah. I painted on top of the canvas. Then they stretched it, photographed it, and ran it as an ad.

RM: Did they showcase it as a Ro-Starr painting?

RO-STARR: Well, it was a collaboration, because the shoe was part of it, but I got my proper credit.

RM: And you felt comfortable with that, because they're paying you, and you respect the company?

RO-STARR: Yeah. I respect Gravis and Burton, the parent company. It was a campaign involving other artist friends of mine as well. They wanted to combine two different elements to serve a purpose.

RM: In combining the two, does that dilute each element, or does the combination create something more powerful?

RO-STARR: Well, it's both. It promotes my art work, and at the same time, it helps Gravis hit a different market—a more urban youth market. And they're trying to push art, which is a pretty new thing. Most athletic companies never really do that.

RM: Showcasing art for a younger audience is definitely a positive thing. Why would a company like Gravis sponsor an artist instead of an athlete?

RO-STARR: I guess that urban youth market is really into a lot of different things now, not necessarily just sports. I mean, they usually advertise sports, and they show a skater in action and all that, but that has all been done before. So, I guess they're really just trying to trail-blaze a new avenue for contemporary art and commercialism, or…How would you call what we do? Is it contemporary? Is it urban? Do we really want to use that word?

RM: I'm not sure it matters.

RO-STARR: We're representing a different movement—the art work we all do, you know. We're kind of well-known within certain communities. So, Gravis really just wants to capture this vibe and repackage it. This makes them look good.

RM: It makes Gravis look good, but how does it

make you look?

RO-STARR: Well, I think it makes the artist look good too. People get to know who I am and get to see my art work. If I look bad to anyone, I guess they would have to walk a mile in my shoes to understand.

RM: What other corporations have you worked with?

RO-STARR: I work with Agnés B.

RM: In what way?

RO-STARR: With Agnés B., I am co-curating a show in Paris at her gallery, I have done painting installations for her Sport B stores in Paris, as well as hand-customizing hats for her 2003 spring/summer collection. It's more than collaborating; she supports artists. It's a patronage thing. She wants artists who she likes to keep pushing the envelope and expressing themselves—whether it's by doing art shows or publishing books for them. No advertising, either. I'll even do a t-shirt for her.

RM: But t-shirts are over, haven't you heard?

RO-STARR: I know, I know, t-shirts are dead. But I'm always going to wear t-shirts. I think it's more that the "limited-edition" thing is over—that kind of Japanese marketing style is kind of played out. But only in our eyes, you know. It's just because we've been doing it with companies for such a long time.

RM: Yeah, I'm tired of it. It's funny how companies want to appear as if they're making "limited-edition" shit.

RO-STARR: It makes people feel like, "Oh shit, I have to get this, because there's not that many, and it's hard to find, and it's like having a piece of gold dust." It's gold dust, it's not a brick of gold,

but it's a piece of it.

RM: What does "limited edition" really mean anymore? It means nothing unless you attach a number to it. You see the phrase used all the time, but it's meaningless unless you know what that edition really is.

RO-STARR: It means "minimum risk," or "limited risk." In collaborating with an artist, it's a kind-of promotion for marketing's sake. What the company wants is something totally different from what the artist really wants. The artists want exposure and respect and to make money.

RM: I would hope that the artists are primarily concerned with making good work.

RO-STARR: Exactly. But not all artists produce good work. A lot of artists don't even know what goal they want to reach, except for being famous and rich. Everything in between is kind-of hard to figure out for the average artist. It's not that simple; it can be very complicated.

RM: I don't know, man. I don't think it's that complicated at all. Concentrate on the work. That's all that really matters.

RO-STARR: I guess that just comes with experience. Commercialism makes people feel like if you're not in a magazine, then you're not doing anything. Or, if you're not on TV, then you haven't made it yet, you know? I also think, going back to the Japanese marketing thing, they really kind of tranquilize the whole country with that "limited-edition" thing and by working with artists. People are becoming very picky about what they spend their money on. So, if it's something that's limited and it's a piece of art, then people are going to think twice about buying it.

RM: The market for these things tends to be

younger people who don't have a lot of money.

RO-STARR: Yeah, I guess that's why artist t-shirts became more popular. There are a handful of people who really spend serious money on art. I guess the art industry wants their world to be exclusive. They don't want it to be for everyone. That's how they secure value, which sucks. I mean, it puts those artists in a weird position, where they have to stay within certain guidelines. I really don't give a fuck about industry guidelines. I want to create my own guidelines and direction. My art needs to be seen, and I'll put my own value on it. Times are definitely changing, and art is changing. That's why it's hard to know exactly what's going on and how to treat it, because it's all so new. So, if you can make art more affordable, the way Keith Haring thought... He opened the Pop Shop because he was really a people person. He didn't really want to make his work so exclusive.

RM: Do you think we're working in that tradition?

RO-STARR: I think we're influenced by that tradition and try to make art more accessible. We're all sons and daughters of Warhol, Haring, etc. We're children of the '80s.

RM: What other projects have you worked on?

RO-STARR: I'm working on a Nike project for Asia, which I consider more of a collaboration of ideas.

RM: It's a commission, right?

RO-STARR: Commission or collaboration. It's for a print and TV campaign as well as for basketball tournaments throughout Asia.

RM: So you're creating art work for the ad campaign, and for the basketball, and for some animation?

RO-STARR: Oh yeah, and I have my own signature basketball too.

RM: How do the two names, Ro-Starr and Nike, appear on the work?

RO-STARR: My name's not on there, but it's in my signature style. People will know that it's my work if they see it, if they know my work. And if they don't, I guess they'll go to the web site and they'll find out more about the project.

RM: This is an example of, not licensing existing art work, but...?

RO-STARR: I created new art work for the project, based on a painting they felt inspired by. But it was really to solve a problem for them. It wasn't just, here's my painting, and there's a shoe next to it. They wanted me to include basketball players that were very recognizable silhouettes within my abstract shapes, and you know, that's kind-of a hard thing to do. Most artists probably wouldn't want to do that.

RM: You're interested in helping them solve their problem, in exchange for...?

RO-STARR: Style is not the only way to solve a problem. I'm more interested in solving a problem based on what the question is. I give up a little of what I want to achieve a middleground. What they provide is good PR and money.

RM: It seems like this project would be more appropriate for an illustrator, since you're providing a service. I suppose they are taking a risk, to a degree, with your work.

RO-STARR: Yeah, for them to go more abstract.

RM: Have you gotten any reactions from your collectors who see your work in ad campaigns? What are the consequences of your work being used in advertising?

RO-STARR: Well, it's hard to say. I get some criticism for working with commercial sponsors like Gravis. That's probably the one advert that people have seen the most, because it was in every single urban fashion magazine around the world. They just pumped it. That makes me feel a little insecure sometimes, because I feel that I'm not being true to myself as an artist. It's a very hard balance. But I don't really give a shit what other people think, to be honest with you. It's like Takashi Murakami working with Louis Vuitton, right? I don't think there's any artist out there on any level who wouldn't work with Louis Vuitton right now.

RM: I don't know. I don't carry a purse or a manbag, or whatever, so I don't know if it'd be a good match for me. Murakami interviewed me on his radio show when I was in Tokyo, and I asked him about that whole Louis Vuitton deal, because I really wanted to get into it. But he didn't want to talk about it at all. Go figure. Has there been an instance where you've seen an artist working for a company and it changed your opinion of the artist or the company?

RO-STARR: Yeah, it's happened. I've seen it many times in magazines, where I felt like, you know, that's way too commercial and playing that artist out. But then, I'll just look at myself and think, well, I did a commercial thing before, too, and maybe there's another person who feels the same exact way about me. It sucks when sponsorship becomes trendy, where companies want to support artists.

RM: Or they want to give the appearance that they're supporting artists.

RO-STARR: Yeah, the façade, because that's the new thing to do.

RM: And throw out terms like "limited edition."

RO-STARR: Exactly. I meet with many buyers in Japan, and whenever they see something that says "limited edition" on it from America, they just start to laugh. It's like a little inside joke, ha ha ha, you know it's not limited. They're saying that just to say it.

RM: And other companies you've worked with?

RO-STARR: Levi's, Royal Elastics, Yamaha, for instance. We were both involved with Royal Elastics in a show called *Street Wise One*, where they paid for the catalog to get made, paid for the space, flew people to London, did press—the whole nine yards. It was a decent show, but after I returned to New York, I'm left kind of unsure looking at the promotional materials. At the end of the day, it's "Royal Elastics' Street Wise One Show," and that's too overt. I've never met with the Royal Elastics people, and I don't really know the product that well. They just make shoes, what does that have to do with art?

RM: That was an odd thing to be involved in.

RO-STARR: Yeah, it's a bit odd.

RM: What did you do with Levi's?

RO-STARR: I've been involved in a few Levi's sponsored events, where they have put money into a show, for flying artists down to Miami for the *Extensions of the Spectacle* show, as well as paying for hotel rooms. With other events, they just wanted their logo hung up on a banner and put on the flyer; that's it. They really wanted us to wear Levi's while we were painting, but we said no, and they didn't mind.

RM: This was a live painting event?

RO-STARR: Yeah, this was at the *Winter Music Conference*. There was also a magazine sponsor and Gravis. Levi's was one of the main sponsors.

RM: What about the Yamaha project?

RO-STARR: The project I was involved in was called *Final Modification I & II*. The artists did the final modification on Jet-skis and motor scooters. It isn't something that Yamaha will produce on a mass scale, only for concept. There were also 3 large paintings 15' x 30' that each artist showcased. The shows were held at X-Realm, Yamaha's gallery in Tokyo. I liked this collaboration a lot, because, we're getting taken care of and a functional sculpture gets produced.

RM: Have you had any sponsorship relationships that have gone sour?

RO-STARR: I definitely protect myself enough so that I've never had it happen that things went really sour.

RM: Because you ask the right questions along the way?

RO-STARR: I know what I want and I have the ability to be flexible, and I make sure everything is in writing. If I'm not happy, I'll just tell them I'm not going to do that. I've been lucky in that I've been looking out for myself. I see other artists working with companies and I know it's hard to be both a business person and an artist at the same time. Working with corporate sponsors, sometimes the vision of the artist gets a little mixed up with the sponsor's vision.

RM: A lot of times it's difficult to separate the art work from the advertising message. You have to be careful about aligning yourself with good companies.

RO-STARR: You must always read between the lines and protect your interests, because no one else will. Companies have to stay on top of the competition, and we're like chess pieces being saved for that right moment. On the positive side, I guess they want someone who's going to speak to that 15- to 30-year old demographic.

RM: And you're the man.

RO-STARR: I guess I am, in that sense.

RM: But you also allow yourself to be that person.

RO-STARR: Yeah, and it's a trade-off.